Entertainment Tourism

Entertainment tourism has recently become more popular. Entertainment attractions encourage tourists to travel around the world to have fun and are an important part of many gaming destinations. This book explores the tourist experience in entertainment destinations. It introduces and outlines the concept of entertainment and tourism in the global environment, focusing on entertainment tourism development in Las Vegas, USA and Macau, China. Macau has become one of the most famous gaming destinations in the world, now surpassing Las Vegas in terms of gaming revenue. This book explores the market for entertainment tourism and major trends, such as Virtual Reality, as well as the experience of tourists using entertainment products.

This book is a valuable resource not only for social science researchers, but also for those in related fields, such as entertainment service providers and tourism officers, among many others.

Jian Ming Luo is an assistant professor in the Faculty of International Tourism and Management at the City University of Macau.

Chi Fung Lam is a tutor at The Chinese University of Hong Kong.

Routledge Focus in Tourism

The *Routledge Focus in Tourism Series* offers a forum for cutting edge research on a wide range of topics and issues within tourism studies. The series provides a forum for short topics aimed at specialized audiences and in-depth case studies that draw on a particular geographic locale. The format for the series is distinctive: each Focus is longer than a journal article and shorter than a traditional monograph.

1   **Entertainment Tourism**
    Jian Ming Luo and Chi Fung Lam

Entertainment Tourism

**Jian Ming Luo and
Chi Fung Lam**

LONDON AND NEW YORK

First published 2018
by Routledge

2 Park Square, Milton Park, Abingdon, Oxfordshire OX14 4RN
52 Vanderbilt Avenue, New York, NY 10017

Routledge is an imprint of the Taylor & Francis Group, an informa business

First issued in paperback 2019

British Library Cataloguing-in-Publication Data
A catalogue record for this book is available from the British Library

Library of Congress Cataloging-in-Publication Data
A catalog record for this book has been requested

ISBN: 978-1-138-06107-1 (hbk)
ISBN: 978-0-367-88917-3 (pbk)

Typeset in Times New Roman
by Apex CoVantage, LLC

Contents

List of figures   vi
List of tables   vii
Preface   viii
Acknowledgements   ix

1 An introduction to entertainment tourism   1

2 History of entertainment tourism   9

3 Entertainment tourism development   17

4 Entertainment tourism management   28

5 Trends of entertainment tourism   35

6 Entertainment product evaluation: a case of tourist
   experience in Macau   42

Index   63

List of figures

1.1   Entertainment-based tourism   3
1.2   Entertainment zones in London   6
2.1   Wynn Macau   14
3.1   Cinema in Galaxy Macau   20
6.1   New entertainment company statistics in Macau   44
6.2   Importance–Performance Analysis grid   47
6.3   Important-Performance Analysis for entertainment products
       in Macau   54

List of tables

2.1 Las Vegas visitor spending profile   10
3.1 An overview of entertainment tourism activities in Macau   21
6.1 Entertainment products in Macau   48
6.2 The demographic profile of respondents   50
6.3 Total number of entertainment product items experienced
     by tourists   52
6.4 Total number of entertainment product categories
     experienced by tourists   53
6.5 Mean scores of entertainment products in importance and
     performance (satisfaction)   53

Preface

Entertainment tourism is becoming more popular nowadays. It encourages tourists to travel around the world to have fun. Entertainment includes popular performing arts, such as concerts, musicals, magic performances, dancing performances, and so on. Entertainment activities are tourism products that are created to satisfy the needs of tourists and to create an unforgettable experience. Entertainment is an important part of many gambling destinations. Gambling, when combined with entertainment, creates a fascinating image and products for the gambling business.

During the last two decades, the entertainment and tourism services industries have undergone major transformations. The entertainment industry is a vast entity featuring numerous categories of entertainment, which includes more than merely venue-based entertainment. Indeed, broadcast media, the Internet, and computer games are just some aspects of the entertainment industry that do not take place in entertainment venues and are therefore not a part of the tourism industry. However, one cannot deny that there is a strong relationship between the two industries.

Chapter 1 is a general introduction to the concept of entertainment and tourism development in the global environment. Chapter 2 is a historical review, focusing on entertainment tourism development in Las Vegas and Macau. Chapter 3 discusses the importance of entertainment in tourism development, particularly in Macau. In Chapter 4, the entertainment tourism market will be discussed. Chapter 5 describes the trends of entertainment tourism. Chapter 6 investigates the importance and performance of the entertainment products in Macau from the customers' perspective. The questionnaire used was designed and analyzed using IPA analysis. This case study will provide a practical perspective on the development of entertainment products in Macau.

Acknowledgements

We would like to thank several people and organizations for their support in the production of this book. Thank you to the Faculty of International Tourism and Management at the City University of Macau for providing the right intellectual environment for ensuring this book was developed and completed. Thanks also go to The Chinese University of Hong Kong and Macau Foundation.

We deeply appreciate an impressive group of colleagues and friends – including but not limited to Professor Hanqin Qiu, Dr. Ka Yin Chau, Dr. Huawen Shen, and Iok Teng Kou – for their support, advice, and guidance. We are also grateful to our graduate students, Guoqiong Huang, Yuangang Zhang, Haonan Chen, and Xiang Cheng. Their help and contributions in maintaining the quality of this book are greatly appreciated. Without their support, this book would not have been accomplished.

Finally, thanks to our families and partners for their love and support in all our endeavors. Without them, we would not have been able to complete this book.

Jian Ming Luo
Chi Fung Lam
Hong Kong, China
August 2017

1   An introduction to entertainment tourism

Defining entertainment tourism

Entertainment tourism has attracted attention from industry and academics (Adeboye, 2012). There are many entertainment products, such as talk shows, concerts, magic performances, dance performances, and so on. Different scholars understand entertainment tourism differently. On one hand, Hughes (2000) defined entertainment as a subset of art performance. On the other hand, Xu (2010) believed that entertainment was a subset of tourism products with the objective of providing an unforgettable experience. Gambling is one of the entertainment products. It provides joy and enhances the attractiveness of a place (Loi & Pearce, 2012). According to McCarthy (2002), gambling is one of the driving forces for economic growth in many countries.

Entertainment is one of the attractions on many tours. Despite the fact that tourism and entertainment are two different industries, both industries share some common areas. Mathieson and Wall (1982) defined tourism as "temporary movement to destinations outside the normal home and workplace, the activities undertaken during the stay, and the facilities created to cater for the need of tourists" (p. 1). According to this definition, the tourism industry includes travel agents and operators, transportation and the associated facilities, hotel accommodations, and site attractions.

Attractions are an important part of the tourism industry. Attractions allow tourists to explore the sights, infrastructures, and wonders of a place. Attractions include but are not limited to arcades, art museums, heritage sites, zoos, parks, botanical gardens, cultural attractions, casinos, and so forth. Some hotels in Southern Europe include entertainment shows to increase the attractiveness of the hotel. The goal is to impress the customers, which can be achieved via the services provided by the hotel, and to make the money paid by the customers worthwhile.

Recreation and entertainment activities include bird watching, fishing, horse riding, golfing, and educational visits to entertainment spots. These facilities hire workers to maintain, manage, operate, and promote the facilities. Hence, recreation and entertainment has become one of the fastest-growing industries in the world. According to the Hospitality Industry Education Advisory Committee (2016), the expected labor hired from this industry is over 20,000 annually.

The attractiveness of a destination comes from different sources, one of which is the perceived ability of a destination to fulfill and satisfy tourists' needs. Mayo and Jarvis (1981) related destination attractiveness to the decision-making process and the associated happiness. In particular, destination attractiveness was defined as a consolidation of travel benefits and the perceived travel benefits of traveling to the particular destination. As individuals thought the destination was able to deliver on their needs, they would become more attracted to the destination and would identify the place as a potential travel destination (Hu & Ritchie, 1993).

Attractions are not only a crucial part of tourism, but also are the driving force of tourism. According to Robinson, Lück, Smith, Lackey (2013, p. 3), tourist attractions are:

> The most important component in the tourism system. They are the main motivators for tourist trips and are the core of the tourism product. Without attractions, there would be no need for other tourism services. Indeed, tourism as such would not exist if it were not for attractions.

Many tourist attractions are connected to entertainment. For example, some tourist attractions include areas for the audience to engage or attempt to captivate emotions through perceptive stimulations. Most theaters, museums, and historical sites could be classified as tourist attractions, but not all entertainment venues are tourist attractions.

Vogel (2014) defined entertainment as things that could stimulate, encourage, and generate enjoyable distractions. In fact, entertainment could generate more than distractions. It could be fascinating and charming. The corresponding word in Latin, *tenare*, means something that could catch you and your soul. Therefore, even when life is not perfect, entertainment provides something people can enjoy and look forward to. This creates the ultimate reason for demanding entertainment products and services. This is the main characteristic of many entertainment attractions, such as cinemas, sports events, theme parks, and so on (Chen, 2012).

There are many categories within the entertainment industry. Some entertainments do not require any entertainment venues, such as media, Internet, and video games. It would be hard to classify these entertainment activities as tourism. On one hand, tourism provides potential markets to

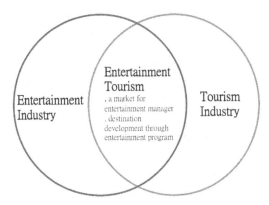

Figure 1.1 Entertainment-based tourism
Source: By authors.

entertainment. On the other hand, the development of tourism depends on entertainment. The parts where the two overlap are entertainment tourism (See Figure 1.1).

The entertainment industry has changed rapidly during the last decade; in particular, the destinations were changing rapidly (Minton, 1998). Entertainment destinations can be defined as places tourists travel to for entertainment activities. The classic example is Branson in Missouri, which was the second most popular destination in the United States in the early 1990s ("Utopia, Missouri", 1994). Recently, entertainment has included a variety of shows, such as concerts, musicals, music and medieval festivals, magic and street performances, circuses, comedy, and so on. Furthermore, other activities, such as sports events, theater, dancing, clubbing, and theme park visits, are also included in entertainment (Besciu, 2013). Las Vegas is another classic example with a particular focus on entertainment activities. The attractions in Las Vegas not only include the casinos, but also live performances. The purpose of the live performances is to lure tourists to stay in the hotel or to gamble in the casino afterwards. Hotels further provide other entertainment products, such as theme parks, virtual reality experiences, and so on (Hughes & Benn, 1997).

Las Vegas provides a wide range of entertainment products, such as nightlife, shows, exhibits, museums, theme parks, pool parties, and so on. In the old days, many hotels included bars, lounges, and showrooms to retain guests. However, ever since Club Rio created the revolutionary first mega nightclub in Las Vegas, the city has been rapidly developing the nightclub business. Various mega nightclubs, such as RA at Luxor, Studio 54 at MGM, Run Jungle at Mandalay Bay, and C2K at the Venetian, were opened afterwards, and Las Vegas developed a whole new market (Stein, 2011). According to Gelt (2011), this business grew at an annual rate of 20% from 2007 to 2011 and became one of the main attractions of the city. Over 40% of visitors claimed to have visited a nightclub, a bar, or a lounge during their stay (Las Vegas Convention and Visitors Authority, LVCVA, 2012).

A profile of the entertainment tourism industry

Tourism and entertainment are two important sectors in the service industry. On one hand, international tourist arrival has grown steadily. There were roughly 25 million international tourist arrivals in 1951, and this number increased to over 500 million in 1995 and over 1 billion in 2015. Furthermore, roughly 10% of the jobs in the world come from the tourism sector, and around 30% of international exports of services come from tourism (UNWTO, 2016). On the other hand, the entertainment sector is an important part of international business. The revenue generated from the entertainment and media market globally was close to USD 1.6 trillion in 2013 and was forecasted to reach USD 2.1 trillion in 2017 (Bond, 2013). In the United States, people spend over USD 200 billion a year on entertainment (Chen, 2012). These numbers have increased academics' and practitioners' attention. In particular, they want to know the functions of the two industries, the relationships between the two industries, and the role played by the service industry under these contexts, which involves much intangible and emotional content (Klassen, Russell, & Chrisman, 1998).

Entertainment tourism is becoming more popular these days (Adeboye, 2012). It encourages tourists to travel around the world to have fun. Entertainment includes popular performing arts, such as concerts, musicals, magic performances, dancing performances, and so on (Hughes, 2000). Entertainment activities are tourism products created to satisfy the needs of tourists and to create an unforgettable experience (Xu, 2010). Entertainment is an important part of many gambling destinations. Gambling, when combined with entertainment, creates a fascinating image and products for the gambling business (Loi & Pearce, 2012). This combination has become the vehicle for economic growth in destinations such as Singapore, the United States, Australia, and Europe. Furthermore, this combination has been used as a repositioning strategy for destinations that depend heavily on gambling (McCarthy, 2002).

Live entertainment is an additional attraction to tourists. People sometimes travel abroad to watch live shows or performances. This action is not limited to international travel, but also includes domestic travel. For example, in 2010, two Finnish girls traveled all the way from Western Finland to Helsinki, a place in Eastern Finland, to watch a live performance. This activity is classified as domestic tourism (Goeldner & Ritchie, 2012). Big concerts attract both domestic and international tourists, which creates demand for short term accommodation during those periods.

Entertainment zones are defined as nightlife areas located at former commercial or industrial areas, underutilized retail corridors, and underdeveloped waterfront. These areas are a by-product of the growth of greedy developments, such as corporate skyscrapers, freeways, parking lots, and mega retail chain stores. They exist around areas such as museums, convention centers, stadiums, and casinos. This urban nightlife is not sophisticated, expensive, and "high-end", limited to the upper class. It is more simple and "down-to-earth" for the general population, who want to drink, dance, and have fun (Campo & Ryan, 2008).

In the United Kingdom, particularly London, tourism is important. In 2015, over 30 million tourists, including domestic and international tourists, traveled to London (VisitBritain, 2016). One particular attraction is the Soho area, which is located in the West End of London. The whole area is only around 3 square kilometers; therefore, walking around the area is feasible. Furthermore, the area is surrounded by Oxford Street, Regent Street, Leicester Square, and Charing Cross Road, which are all famous and popular tourist attractions. Soho in London is famous for live performances, from great musicals to street performance; from great dinners to fascinating nightlife; from popular bars, such as The O Bar and Bar Soho, to casual pubs and secret bars. One can also find great theaters, such as the Prince Edward Theatre and the Prince of Wales Theatre. Until 2015, over 14 million people visited Soho in London and spent over 600 million pounds (see Figure 1.2) (Society of London Theatre, 2016).

In the United States and Italy, there have been many innovations in retail shopping and leisure centers. This is especially true in Italy. According to the Ministry of Industry, over 40% of the total space in shopping centers is allocated to extra-retail services (Ministero delle Attivita' Produttive, 2002). Due to architectural features and synergetic effects, particularly the trinity of synergy among retail, food and beverage, and entertainment, these shopping and leisure centers eventually became tourist attractions and community centers (Beyard, Braun, McLaughlin, Philips, & Rubin, 2001). Furthermore, the integrated features of these shopping and leisure centers allow people to enjoy cinema, restaurants, live performances, exhibitions, and fitness centers all in one safe and weatherproof environment. In Las Vegas, many resorts advocate celebrity chef restaurants, multimillion-dollar shows, boutique shops, nightclubs, and spas. These amenities have become one of the revenue centers of modern resorts (Vora, 2007).

Figure 1.2 Entertainment zones in London
Source: By authors.

In Hong Kong, Lan Kwai Fong is the analogy of Soho in London. It is the most popular nightlife area. There are over 90 restaurants and bars, which offer a huge variety of food and beverages, in this area. Many movies have been filmed in this area, and it is easy to spot celebrities. Furthermore, this area hosts many major festivals and carnivals, such as Halloween, Christmas, New Year's Eve, and its own beer festival (Hong Kong Tourism Board, 2017).

Summary

This chapter was an introduction to entertainment tourism. In the last two decades, both the entertainment industry and the tourism industry have experienced important transformations. The entertainment industry is composed of numerous entities. Entertainment venues, entertainment zones, media, Internet, and computer games are some examples of the industry. While some areas of the entertainment industry are not part of the tourism industry, one cannot deny the strong relationship between the two industries. It is our hope that the remaining chapters will provide you a broader understanding of entertainment tourism.

References

Adeboye, C. A. (2012). *The impact of entertainment on tourism. Case study: Agency Remarc in Greece*. Central Ostrobothnia University of Applied. Retrieved on 02 February 2016, from www.theseus.fi/bitstream/handle/10024/47217/Adeboye_Christopher.pdf?sequence=1

Besciu, I. G. (2013). Behavior of the consumer of tourist entertainment services. *Cactus Tourism Journal, 4*(2), 9–19.

Beyard, M. D., Braun, R. E., McLaughlin, H., Philips, P. L., & Rubin, M. S. (2001). *Developing retail entertainment destinations*. Washington, DC: Urban Land Institute.

Bond, P. (2013, April 06). Study: Global media industry poised to top $2 trillion in 2016. *The Hollywood Reporter*. Retrieved on 02 February 2016, from www.hollywoodreporter.com/news/study-global-media-industry-poised-562694

Campo, D., & Ryan, B. D. (2008). The entertainment zone: Unplanned nightlife and the revitalization of the American downtown. *Journal of Urban Design, 13*(3), 291–315.

Chen, C. K. (2012). Hierarchical linear relationship between the US leisure and entertainment consumption. *Technology in Society, 34*(1), 44–54.

Gelt, J. (2011, June 24). Las Vegas: Bright lights, dance city. *Los Angeles Times*. Retrieved on 02 February 2016, from http://articles.latimes.com/2011/jun/24/entertainment/la-et-las-vegas-electronica-20110624

Goeldner, C. R., & Ritchie, J. B. (2012). *Tourism: Principles, practices, philosophies*, 12th ed. Hoboken, NJ: John Wiley and Sons, Inc.

Hong Kong Tourism Board. (2017). *Things to do*. Retrieved on 20 March 2017, from www.discoverhongkong.com/us/dine-drink/where-to-eat/lan-kwai-fong.jsp

Hospitality Industry Education Advisory Committee. (2016). *Entertainment and tourism*. Retrieved on 02 February 2016, from www.go2hr.ca/bc-tourism-industry/what-tourism/recreation-and-entertainment

Hu, Y., & Ritchie, J. B. (1993). Measuring destination attractiveness: A contextual approach. *Journal of Travel Research, 32*(2), 25–34.

Hughes, H. (2000). *Arts, entertainment and tourism*. Oxford: Butterworth Heinemann.

Hughes, H., & Benn, D. (1997). Tourism and cultural policy: The case of seaside entertainment in Britain. *European Journal of Cultural Policy, 3*(2), 235–255.

Klassen, K. J., Russell, R. M., & Chrisman, J. J. (1998). Efficiency and productivity measures for high contact services. *Service Industries Journal, 18*(4), 1–18.

Las Vegas Convention and Visitors Authority. (2012). *Las Vegas visitor profile study 2011*. Retrieved on 02 February 2016, from www.lvcva.com/includes/content/images/mdia/docs/2011-Las_Vegas_Visitor_profile.pdf

Loi, K. I., & Pearce, P. L. (2012). Powerful stakeholders' views of entertainment in Macao's future. *Journal of Business Research, 65*(1), 4–12.

Mathieson, A., & Wall, G. (1982). *Tourism, economic, physical and social impacts*. London: Longman.

Mayo, E. J., & Jarvis, L. P. (1981). *The psychology of leisure travel: Effective marketing and selling of travel services*. Boston: CBI Publishing Company.

McCarthy, J. (2002). Entertainment-led regeneration: The case of Detroit. *Cities, 19*(2), 105–111.

Ministero delle Attivita' Produttive. (2002). *Rapporto sugli aspetti strutturali del sistema distributivo italiano*. Rome: Ministero delle Attivita' Produttive.

Minton, E. (1998). For your amusement: What the entertainment industry is doing for places large and small. *Planning, 64*(9), 12–15.

Robinson, P., Lück, M., Smith, S. L., & Lackey, M. (Eds.). (2013). *Tourism*. CABI.

Society of London Theatre. (2016). *The box office data report 2015*. Retrieved on 17 March 2017, from http://solt.co.uk/about-london-theatre/facts-and-figures/

Stein, M. (2011, December 22). *Las Vegas nightlife timeline*. Seven. Retrieved from www.weeklyseven.com/feature/2011/12/22/las-vegas-nightlife-timeline

UNWTO. (2016). *UNWTO world tourism barometer*. Retrieved from http://media.unwto.org/press-release/2016-01-18/international-tourist-arrivals-4-reach-record-12-billion-2015

"Utopia, Missouri" (1994, December 24). *The Economist, 333*, 25–29.

VisitBritain. (2016). *Inbound research & insights*. Retrieved on 01 March 2017, from www.visitbritain.org/inbound-research-insights

Vogel, H. L. (2014). *Entertainment industry economics: A guide for financial analysis*. Cambridge: Cambridge University Press.

Vora, S. (2007, May 31). *In pictures: Las Vegas' most luxurious spots*. Retrieved from www.forbes.com/2007/05/30/vegas-casino-luxury-forbeslife-cx_sv_0531travel_slide.html

Xu, J. B. (2010). Perception of tourism products. *Tourism Management, 31*, 607–610.

2 History of entertainment tourism

Las Vegas: Western entertainment tourism

Brief history of Las Vegas

Las Vegas was formed as a city in 1905. The downtown area in Las Vegas, the Strip, was originally land besides the Union Pacific Railroad tracks. Nevada was the first state among all states in the United States to legalize gambling. Ever since then, the state has been under the spotlight of the world. After the Second World War, numerous hotels, casinos, and internationally recognized entertainments invaded Las Vegas. As more corporations, such as Howard Hughes, entered the entertainment business via purchasing hotel-casino properties, gambling (which was also known as gaming) gradually transitioned into a legitimate business.

Tourism represents a huge proportion of Nevada's economy. Under the umbrella of tourism, gaming is the largest revenue-generating industry and one of the largest revenue generators of the entertainment sector in the United States. From the 1960s to 1980s, Las Vegas grew to become an internationally recognized city – or infamously, the "Sin City" – for gaming, shows, and nightlife. Starting from the 1990s, hotels and entertainment complexes targeting family fun opened. These hotels and entertainment complexes might include water theme parks and family-oriented restaurants, theater, and children's programs. In 2003, the Las Vegas Convention and Visitors Authority (LVCVA) promoted the city with the slogan "What happens in Vegas, stays in Vegas". The slogan meant that people could come to Vegas to do whatever they wanted (conditional on its legality) in confidence. Different slogans were released afterwards. However, this slogan was one of the most famous. In 2009, the old "What happens" marketing theme was brought back, with some adjustments in 2010 for the post-recession consumer (Velotta, 2010).

In 1989, Steve Wynn invested over USD 500 million to build the first mega-casino resort, the Mirage. As the project went over budget, the final investment totaled over USD 600 million (Kim, 2010). The windows of the hotel are colored gold. This color originated from the idea of gold dust from the tinting process. The hotel has held numerous shows, such as Siegfried & Roy, Nouvelle Expérience, LOVE, and so on. Furthermore, the hotel built notable attractions, such as Siegfried & Roy's Secret Garden and Dolphin Habitat, an artificial volcano, an atrium, a huge aquarium, 1OAK nightclub, Revolution Ultra Lounge, and Bare. As more internationally recognized hotel brands, such as the AXIS, Las Vegas Festival Grounds, the Colosseum at Caesars Palace, Mandalay Bay Events Center, MGM Grand Garden Arena, T-Mobile Arena, Tryst Nightclub, and XS Nightclub, entered the Strip, the Las Vegas Strip became the center for world entertainment.

Before 1992, most of the casinos (over 80%) in Las Vegas were concentrated in the Strip. Las Vegas began to develop a new attraction, the Fremont Street Experience, to attract visitors. The Fremont Street Experience opened in 1995. This canopied, five-block area features 12.5 million LED lights and 550,000 watts of sound from dusk until midnight, especially during shows held on the top of each hour.

Nowadays, Las Vegas has been named "The Entertainment Capital of the World" (Macy, 1991) and has become one of the most popular destination in the world (International Trade Administration, US Department of Commerce, 2014). Las Vegas provides a broad scope of entertainment options including nightlife, shows, exhibits, museums, theme parks, pool parties, and so on. Particularly, nightclubs are considered the highlight of Las Vegas. Furthermore, nightclubs have generated significant revenue even during the period of recession. The growth rate between 2007 and 2010 was 20% (Gelt, 2011). Besides gaming and nightclubs, live entertainment has grown to be another important revenue source for the tourism industry. In 2016, the tax revenue generated from the live entertainment industry reached 109 million (LVCVA, 2017).

Table 2.1 Las Vegas visitor spending profile (2016, USD)

Category	Per Visit	Annual Total
Room	$122	$5,249,156,119
Food and beverage	$91	$3,890,540,567
Local transportation	$96	$4,125,301,353
Shopping	$157	$6,737,104,863
Live entertainment	$68	$2,900,334,163
Sightseeing	$36	$1,542,694,396
Gaming	$177	$7,605,313,523
Other	$80	$3,441,306,256

Source: Las Vegas Convention and Visitors Authority, 2017.

Las Vegas: the entertainment capital of the world

The entertainment industry in Vegas began with a few headline casinos built around Highway 91 (Macy, 1991). As gambling became legal, the city underwent a huge development. Starting in the early 1980s, the development of Vegas went hand-in-hand with the national economy. Initially, the town was an "adult playground" that offered legal gambling, showgirls, and headliners. However, as the national economy suffered a financial crisis, the city experienced a similar downturn during the same period. Tourist numbers dropped, and the locals were not coming. As more places, such as Deadwood, South Dakota; Central City, Colorado; and even land owned by American Indians, legalized gambling, gambling could be found everywhere in America. Therefore, Las Vegas needed to find a way to rebuild its prosperity (Toewe, 2013). One strategy was to develop the international tourist market. Hence, the city was developed to make it more assessable to international tourists. To resolve the language problem of international tourists, the city adopted visual communication instead of written or oral communication. To attract local residents and more common American families, the "adult only" reputation needed to be replaced.

Spectacle environment – overcoming language barriers

As Las Vegas began to attract international tourists, language problems had to be resolved. To address such language barriers, the entertainment gurus of Las Vegas created an environment of non-verbal spectacle, providing visual stimulation through lights, animation, colors, symbols, and images.

Family-oriented attractions – no longer adults only

Originally, the adult entertainment in Las Vegas provided women to "serve" their customers. However, these kinds of activities were not suitable for children and hence limited the amount of visitation. Later on, Circus Casino offered some family fun options, but it did not provide lodging for its visitors. Steve Wynn eventually created resorts that included more family attractions, such as the wildlife habitat at the Mirage and the pirate themed Treasure Island.

Entertainment climate – intersected products

During the same period, Cirque du Soleil, a circus from Montreal, was developing new markets. The needs of Las Vegas and Cirque du Soleil coincided. Cirque du Soleil finally opened its first show, Mystère, at the Mirage in 1993. Since its performances used limited words, it matched the aforementioned spectacle environment, the language barrier. Besides that, the local residents were attracted by this show. As there was a double coincidence of wants, Cirque du Soleil and Las Vegas became a perfect match. This also changed the circumstances of the entertainment industry in Las Vegas. Due to its family-friendly style, international appeal, and wordless shows, Cirque du Soleil became a great success. Today, there are seven residential shows from Cirque du Soleil in Las Vegas. They are Mystère, "O", Zumanity, KA, Criss Angel MINDFREAK, The Beatles LOVE, and Michael Jackson ONE (Cirquedusoleil.com, 2017). According to the Cirque, the goal was to develop a new show in every MGM hotel and, hopefully, to extend the shows to other properties. In 2016, over 40% of tourists went to a lounge act during their stay in Vegas, 32% of tourists visited a Broadway show, and 24% of tourists visited a headliner (Statista, 2017). From this perspective, Cirque du Soleil changed the culture of entertainment in Vegas. This further induced interest from academics. For example, Walsh (2006) studied how the Broadway musical in New York evolved and integrated to entertainment in Vegas to fulfill the specific needs of the audience.

Macau: Asian entertainment tourism

The history of Macau

Macau, also known as Macao or Ou Mun, was an autonomous territory located on the border of Zhuhai, on the east of Hong Kong, and on the west of the Pearl River Delta (PRD). The name Ou Mun was because of its location at the mouth of PRD. The official name was Macao Special Administrative Region of the People's Republic of China. In 2016, the population of Macau was around 650,000 and the area was around 30 square kilometers. It was one of the most densely populated regions in the world (Macao's Statistics and Census Service [DSEC], 2017). Portuguese were the first to settle in Macau in the 1550s. The Portuguese adopted the name Ou Mun, which gradually changed into the name Macao. With the permission of Guangdong's mandarins, the Portuguese established the city, which within a short time had become a major mid-point stop for trade between China, Japan, India, and Europe. As well, Macau had become a favorite destination for international tourists (Macao Government Tourism Office, 2017). In 1557, Macau became a colony of Portugal under a mutual agreement between China and Portugal. The agreement was extended to 1999. Macau eventually became part of China on 20 December 1999. Since then, Macau had become a special administrative region according to the Joint Declaration on the Question of Macau and Macau Basic Law (DSEC, 2017).

In the past, the main industries in Macau were textiles, electronics, and toys. However, after many years, tourism became the dominant industry in Macau. There are now a wide variety of luxury hotels, resorts, Meetings, Incentives, Conferencing, Exhibitions (MICE) facilities, restaurants, and casinos. Macau's economy is closely linked to the economy of Hong Kong and Guangdong Province, in particular the Pearl River Delta region. Macau qualifies as one of Asia's "little tigers". Furthermore, Macau also provides financial and banking services, staff training, transport, and communications support.

Macau, as a Special Administrative Region of China, enjoyed "one country, two systems", which allowed Macau to be ruled under great autonomy. As the region grows in size, infrastructure, and economy, the region also possessed unique features, such as the integration of Portuguese and Chinese culture. This has created a unique characteristic attractive to many international tourists. Since 2006, it has generated the largest gaming revenue in the world. Despite its concentration in the gaming business, it has the fourth highest life expectancy in the world and is one of the regions in Asia with a "very high Human Development Index" (World Bank, 2015). Macau was also one the world's richest regions, measured in terms of GDP per capita (World Bank, 2015).

Entertainment tourism in Macau

In 1962, the Macau government issued a monopoly license of gambling to Stanley Ho's Sociedade de Turismo e Diversões de Macau (STDM). Starting in 2002, the Macau government terminated the monopoly and invited others to participate. After a period of bidding and negotiation, six casino concessions and subconcessions were allocated to STDM, Wynn Macau, Las Vegas Sands, Galaxy Entertainment Group, the partnership of MGM Mirage and Pansy Ho (daughter of Stanley Ho), and the partnership of Melco and Publishing and Broadcasting Limited (PBL). Nowadays, STDM owns the largest number of casinos, 16 casinos in total, in Macau. In 2004, as Sands Macau entered the market, the gaming industry of Macau entered into a new era. Following Sands Macau, Wynn Macau, MGM Grand, the Venetian Macau, and Galaxy Cotai Megaresort entered the market in 2006, 2007, and 2011 respectively (see Figure 2.1). Another megaresort, Lisboa Palace, was expected to be completed and open in 2017. According to the Gaming Inspection and Coordination Bureau, DICJ (2017), the revenue generated from gambling in Macau surpasses Las Vegas.

As Macau terminated the gaming monopoly in the last decade, the Macau government and the Chinese government began encouraging the economy to diversify the overly concentrated gaming industry, especially after the decrease of tourist arrivals during the financial crisis in 2008. According to the 12th Five-Year Plan, the Chinese government supported Macau's

Figure 2.1 Wynn Macau
Source: By authors.

establishment as the "World Tourism and Leisure Center". Furthermore, the Guangdong-Macau Cooperation Framework Agreement stated that "Macau is expected to transform from a largely casino gaming city to a more family and business travel destination" (Cohen, 2011). The goal was to diversify the existing market and develop new markets as well as new attractions. However, the attempt was not successful as the growth rate from non-gaming revenue was significantly lower than the growth from gaming revenue (Cohen, 2011).

Summary

This chapter described the evolution of entertainment tourism through a comparison of two major entertainment cities in the world, Las Vegas and Macau. On one hand, since Las Vegas has suffered some downfall in terms of the number of visitors throughout the years, the city has expanded its entertainment business with Cirque du Soleil. In fact, this transition was very successful. The city further expanded its diversification to Broadway shows and other headliners. On the other hand, Macau suffered similar problems of tourist downfall in recent years, especially after the financial crisis in 2008. Both the Macau and Chinese governments have been encouraging the diversification of the industry. Since Macau possessed both Chinese and Portuguese culture, this allowed Macau to inherit many holidays, festivals, events, and activities. This should give Macau plenty of opportunities to develop new attractions and markets. However, unfortunately, the growth rate between gaming and non-gaming revenue in recent years provided unsatisfactory evidence of the success of this endeavor.

References

Cirquedusoleil.com. (2017). *Shows by Cirque du Soleil.* Retrieved on 01 May 2017, from www.cirquedusoleil.com/en/shows.aspx

Cohen, M. (2011, June 30). Macau needs decades to go beyond gambling. *Asia Time Online.* Retrieved on 01 February 2016, from www.atimes.com/atimes/Southeast_Asia/MF30Ae02.html

Gaming Inspection and Coordination Bureau (DICJ). (2017). *Macao.* Retrieved on 01 May 2017, from http://www.dicj.gov.mo/web/en/information/index.html

Gelt, J. (2011, June 24). Las Vegas: Bright lights, dance city. *Los Angeles Times.* Retrieved on 01 May 2017, from http://articles.latimes.com/2011/jun/24/entertainment/la-et-las-vegas-electronica-20110624

International Trade Administration, US Department of Commerce. (2014). *Overseas visitation estimates for U.S. states, cities, and census regions: 2013.* Retrieved from http://tinet.ita.doc.gov/outreachpages/download_data_table/2013_States_and_Cities.pdf

Kim, J. E. (2010). *Sunrise, sunset? Comparing the Las Vegas and Macao gaming markets in 2010.* Master's Thesis, University of Nevada, Las Vegas. Retrieved from http://digitalscholarship.unlv.edu/thesesdissertations/652

Las Vegas Convention and Visitors Authority. (2017). *Las Vegas visitor profile study 2016.* Retrieved on 01 May 2017, from www.lvcva.com/includes/content/images/media/docs/2016-Las-Vegas-Visitor-Profile.pdf

Macao Government Tourism Office. (2017). *About Macao.* Retrieved on 01 May 2017, from http://en.macaotourism.gov.mo/plan/aboutmacao_detail.php?id=1

Macao's Statistics and Census Service (DSEC). (2017). *Macao in figures.* Retrieved on 01 May 2017, from www.dsec.gov.mo/Statistic.aspx?NodeGuid=ba1a4eab-213a-48a3-8fbb-962d15dc6f87

Macy, R. (1991). Melinda. In *Destination Baghdad.* Las Vegas, NV: M&M Graphics.

Statista. (2017). *Leading types of entertainment attended by visitors in Las Vegas 2016.* Retrieved on 01 May 2017, from www.statista.com/statistics/411792/types-of-entertainment-las-vegas-visitors-attended-us/

Toewe, A. M. (2013). *"Flowers in the desert": Cirque du Soleil in Las Vegas 1993–2012.* Doctoral dissertation, University of Colorado, Boulder. Retrieved from http://scholar.colorado.edu/cgi/viewcontent.cgi?article=1021&context=thtr_gradetds

Velotta, R. N. (2010). Gaming commission rejects slot machines at cash registers. *Las Vegas Sun,* 18.

Walsh, J. (2006). *Broadway in the desert defining success for the Broadway musical on the Las Vegas strip*. Doctoral dissertation, University of Nevada, Las Vegas.

World Bank. (2015). *Data*. Retrieved on 01 May 2017, from http://data.worldbank. org/indicator/NY.GDP.PCAP.PP.CD?order=wbapi_data_value_2016+wbapi_ data_value+wbapi_data_value-last&sort=desc

3 Entertainment tourism development

The importance of entertainment on tourism development

According to the description of Sternberg (1997), the primary goal of tourism was to sell a "staged" experience and the core productivity of tourism was to create a tourism experience. The physical characteristics of a tourism destination provided less motivation than the mental and emotional "pre-experience", which could be described as the expected experience, to tourists. For example, many people traveled to Madison County in Iowa to visit the bridge where the two lovers in the film *The Bridges of Madison County* kissed, but few people cared about the physical details of the bridge. Ultimately, tourists were seeking experiences that could be provided by the goods and services in the destination. Therefore, many tourism destinations have been targeted to sell an "experience" (Richards, 2001).

Nowadays, tourism has emerged as a huge business, although it evolved from traditional storytelling, gladiator fights, and horse racing. People gained more experiences and knowledge about traveling. People developed clear opinions about where they were about to travel and what they were expecting. The most common expectations of tourists were entertainment and leisure. Furthermore, among the entertainment and leisure category, casinos, popular pubs, bars, discos, clubs, cinemas, and concerts were often cited as reasons for traveling. Since demand for entertainment and leisure has increased, many hotels, particularly hotels in Southern Europe, provide entertainment shows to attract and retain guests.

In 2006, the "crown" of top gambling destination belonging to Las Vegas was taken over by Macau (Rigby, 2008). The entertainment industry in Asia grew, and spending per visitor increased, which proved an excellent time to expand and diversify the entertainment industry in Macau. For example, nightlife entertainment became an important part of and revenue source for gaming markets in Asia. The number of bars, nightclubs, karaokes, and discos reached 200,000 in 2013. The revenue generated exceeded USD 6 billion at the same time. Similar patterns could also be observed in other southeast Asia markets, such as South Korea, the Philippines, Singapore, Malaysia, and Vietnam. Changes in Las Vegas were more severe. Much new revenue was generated from restaurants with famous chefs, shows, fashion/luxury brand shops, nightclubs, and bars (Banay, 2006; Vora, 2007). In the United States, the total amount of hours spent on entertainment reached 140 billion hours annually. The amount spent on entertainment reached USD 280 billion annually. Globally, total annual spending reached USD 1 trillion (Chen, 2012). Due to the increasing contribution of entertainment, many multi-million-dollar projects, such as the Smith Center for the Performing Arts, the DISCOVERY Children's Museum, the Mob Museum, and the Neon Museum, were developed in 2012. The year 2012 was further marked as "The Year of Downtown".

The role of entertainment in tourism became particularly important to casinos. Many casinos provide entertainment properties, such as prominent entertainment-themed and non-gaming outlets. For example, managers at the Hard Rock Hotel tried to create an experience featuring its core entertainment (Jones, 2009). Due to the increasing importance of the entertainment industry, billionaires, such as Jack Ma and Wang Jianlin, have increased their business in the entertainment industry. Despite the recent interest of business toward the entertainment industry, the cooperation or integration between the entertainment industry and tourism started a long time ago (Lucas & Kilby, 2008). Investment in entertainment requires a huge amount of investment. For example, the investment of KA, a Cirque du Soleil show, in MGM Grand reached USD 165 million (Palmeri, 2004b). Similarly, the investment of the Celine Dion show in Caesars Palace reached USD 95 million (Leach, 2013).

Different researchers have different opinions on how entertainment affects tourism. Researchers noted that while, on one hand, the operating profits of a casino amenity could be found easily on the amenity's departmental income statement, on the other hand, the indirect effect of the amenity on other revenue centers within a casino via guest traffic that spills over onto other operations is not evident (Suh, 2006; Suh & Lucas, 2011). As casino resorts invested huge amounts of money on amenities, such as showroom and entertainment venues, it became important to evaluate the direct and indirect contributions of these amenities (Suh & Lucas, 2011). Numerous researchers attempted to evaluate the indirect contribution of these amenities towards gaming or non-gaming business (Lucas, Dunn, & Kharitonova, 2006; Lucas & Santos, 2003; Roehl, 1996; Suh & Lucas, 2011; Suh & West, 2010). There were two main difficulties. Since there were many factors that could affect the gaming volume, the first difficulty was to identify the impact of the contributions from these casino amenities. Furthermore, since many casinos sublet their places to other restaurants, luxury stores, and so on, the second difficulty was to track all spending of guests, even within the same resort (Lucas & Kilby, 2008; Kilby, Fox, & Lucas, 2004; Suh, 2006). Despite these difficulties, based on existing research, the results could be classified into two mainstream theories.

The first theory was full service theory. According to this theory, gambling was seldom the only reason people came to the casino. Therefore, according to this theory, if a casino possessed no amenities, no one would visit that casino (Lucas & Kilby, 2008). The second theory was spillover effects. Based on this theory, people tend to minimize their shopping or cruising time by visiting several stores within the same place (Brueckner, 1993). Therefore, according to this theory, if a casino possessed no amenities, people would still visit that casino. The amenities would only increase the tendency of people to visit casinos.

As we observe from previous chapters, entertainment has changed the casino industry. Entertainment has become a major attraction to not only existing tourists, but also to new customers who enjoy non-gaming activities more than gaming activities. According to an estimation from Benston (2003), entertainment shows contributed 20% of a casino's revenue. Similarly, Suh and West (2010) found a positive relationship between the presence of entertainment shows and gaming volume during the hours close to the show time. The main justification of investing a huge sum of money in non-gaming amenities was the expectation or hope of attracting people visiting casinos (Benston, 2003; Heretakis, 2008; Palmeri, 2004a; Samuels, 1999). In certain situations, casinos might be willing to operate these amenities at a loss and use the revenue generated from the casino to compensate (Atlas, 1995; Christiansen & Brinkerhoff-Jacobs, 1995; Guier, 1999; Lucas & Kilby, 2008; Samuels, 1999; Tiscali Music, 2003; Yoshihashi, 1993). For instance, famous headliner shows, such as Bill Cosby, Harry Connick, Jr., and Frank Sinatra, operated at a 10 million dollar loss annually (Yoshihashi, 1993). However, perhaps the justification of the indirect benefit of the amenities was so significant that many researchers found that many casino amenities report loss or marginal profit (Lucas et al., 2006; Lucas & Kilby, 2008; Lucas & Santos, 2003; Suh & Lucas, 2011).

As resorts integrate more non-gaming activities and amenities, non-gaming revenues are expected to increase. However, several clarifications should be notified. One important clarification is that revenue does not equal profit. According to MacDonald and Eadington (2008), it was profit, instead of revenue, generated from gaming that justified the investment in non-gaming amenities. The use of gaming revenue or profit to subsidize non-gaming amenities is not sustainable. As competition among resorts becomes more fierce, gaming profits may no longer be able to compensate the loss from others. Therefore, Suh and Lucas (2011) suggested that non-gaming amenities should not be a complement of the gaming department. Non-gaming amenities should enhance themselves to become a profit-generating center. When demand for these non-gaming activities increased, the price of these amenities increased (Suh, 2011). Kale (2006) further examined this hypothesis or possibility. The researcher studied the forecasted return on investment between gaming and non-gaming projects in Singapore. However, the researcher found that the return on investment for non-gaming amenities required indirect contributions to the gaming department to justify the investment.

Entertainment tourism development in Macau

Macau entertainment tourism outlook

As mentioned in the previous chapters, Macau opened its gaming sector a decade ago. Ever since, both the Macau and Chinese governments have encouraged Macau to diversify its economy. Regardless of the success of the non-gaming sector, such as the House of Dancing Water at City of Dreams, the revenue generated was not comparable to the revenue from the gaming sector (see Figure 3.1). Furthermore, these non-gaming sectors

Figure 3.1 Cinema in Galaxy Macau
Source: By authors.

were not without risk. For example, ZAiA at Venetian was closed due to lack of visitors. Therefore, investors lack incentives to create similar stage spectacles in what has been a "Macau-see, Macau-do" business culture (Cohen, 2011). Based on statistics from Macau.com, people generally booked non-gambling tickets 6–8 weeks in advance. This did not include last-minute purchases. Generally speaking, people purchased in advance because they worried about limited seats. The average transaction was about 2,500 HKD with at least a two night's stay. This allowed people to catch more shows and entertainment activities. The majority of the visitors were from Hong Kong, South Korea, Taiwan, mainland China, and Singapore. Many visitors also visited other entertainment facilities, such as Taboo at City of Dreams, the Hard Rock Hotel, and other shows at the China Rouge nightclub in Galaxy Macau. Macau was growing into a world-class city with diversified art and cultural exhibits (PRLog, 2013). According to the Macao Government Tourism Office (MGTO), entertainment has become a major factor inducing tourists to visit. According to MGTO, entertainment can be generally classified into shows, cultural and creative industries zones, family fun, sports and recreation, beauty and wellness, gaming, and nightlife (See Table 3.1).

Table 3.1 An overview of entertainment tourism activities in Macau

Type	Examples	
Shows	The House of Dancing Water	Created and directed by Franco Dragone. The total amount of investment of the House of Dancing Water reached USD 250 million. This show expresses Asian culture on a water stage. The main theme of the show is about the "seven emotions" originated from Confucianism.
	Yueju Opera (Cantonese Opera)	Yueju Opera is a Chinese traditional show originated from Guangdong, Guangxi, Hong Kong, and Macau. It is one of the most influential shows in China and was awarded as "Masterpiece of the Oral and Intangible Heritage of Humanity" by UNESCO in September 2009.
	The House of Magic	The House of Magic is a premier venue for magicians around the world. Currently, Franz Harary is the host and one of the performers. The show includes Mega Magics, which is one of Harary's resident shows. This show attracts many visitors to enjoy the amazing magic performed by numerous magicians from around the world.

(*Continued*)

Table 3.1 (Continued)

Type	Examples	
Cultural and creative industries zones	AFA (Art for All Society)	AFA is a non-profit organization established in 2007. The objective is to encourage contemporary art development, local creativity, and local cultural initiatives in Macau. The organization provides space for exhibitions, such as paintings, photography, sculptures, prints, and video.
	Ox Warehouse	Ox Warehouse, originally known as "Old Ladies' House Art Space", was a non-profit art association opened in 2002. The objective of this organization is very similar to AFA, and hence the exhibitions provided are also very similar. However, in addition, it provides drawing and music workshops to adults and children.
	Creative Macau	Creative Macau is a non-profit organization aiming at promoting local creative industries. It provides space for advertising, architecture, crafts, fashion design, film, interactive leisure, music, etc.
Family fun	Macao Giant Panda Pavilion	Macao Giant Panda Pavilion is composed of three main areas, Rare Animal Zone, Seac Pai Van Park, and Flora Garden. The pavilion provide education on animal conservation to local residents and tourists. Seac Pai Van Park is the first country park in Macau and listed zone protected by law. Flora Garden is the only park that possesses an Asian black bear.
	Macao Science Center	The Macao Science Center consists of three main areas, the Exhibition Center, the Planetarium, and the Convention Center. The Exhibition Center is the tallest building in Macau and contains 14 galleries organized in an upward spiral. It is designed by world-renowned Chinese-American architect I. M. Pei. The previous gallery exhibitions include space, children, robotics, acoustics, genetics, etc.
		The Planetarium contains a dome-shaped tilted screen of 15.24 meters in diameter. It is the highest resolution (8,000 x 8,000 pixels) 3D planetarium as listed by Guinness World Records.
	Macau Tower	Macau Tower is one of the landmarks in Macau and is over 330 meters in height. It includes restaurants, theaters, a shopping mall, an observation deck, Skywalk X, etc. Visitors can also try the Skyjump or Bungee jump in the tower, which is the highest commercial skyjump in the world. Or visitors can try the Tower Climb, which allows visitors to climb up to the very top of Macau Tower through an outdoor vertical ladder.

Type	Examples	
Sports and recreation	Karting	For those who enjoy speed, karting in Macau is a must. The kart race on Coloane Island is one of the most difficult tracks in Asia, and it is the only permanent track in Macau or Hong Kong.
	Beaches and nautical sports	One of the most popular beaches in Macau is Hác-Sá Beach. Hác-Sá Beach is one of the "must-see" attractions in Macau. However, due to erosion issues, the area of Hác-Sá Beach is reducing. Hence, the Macau government refills the beach with artificial yellow sand.
Beauty and wellness	Spas	Many five-star hotels in Macao provide excellent spa facilities offering all-natural products and experts versed in leading rejuvenation and relaxation techniques. People can indulge themselves with special spa treatments, massages, health consultations, skincare, nail polish, and facial services for a revolutionary, refreshing rest!
	Medical beauty care	Medical beauty care is a combination of beauty and medicine providing patrons with a new health choice. People can benefit from the medical beauty service to reduce pressure and effectively improve their health following a hectic day.
Gaming	Casinos	In recent years, Macao's gaming industry has been developing at a rapid pace, with a number of larger casinos offering a free direct shuttle bus service to and from border crossings. Many casinos feature international cuisine restaurants, recreational facilities, and top-flight family entertainment as well as gaming.
	Greyhound racing and horse racing	Those who do not enjoy table games or slot machines can try their luck on greyhound or horse racing in Macau. Besides, greyhound racing has a very long history, the beginning of which dates back to 1912. The only greyhound racing stadium in Asia, Canidrome, opened in the 1960s.
Nightlife	Bars and lounges	Most hotels include bars and lounges. Some might include live music and dance performance. Other bars and lounges can be found along Avenida Dr. Sun Yat-Sen, which faces the Outer Harbour. Besides the bars' facilities, one can also enjoy the harbor view.
	Dance clubs	There are many nightclubs in Macau. For example, Club Cubic located at the City of Dreams is the biggest club in Macau. Popular DJs or singers such as PSY, LMFAO, Steve Aoki, etc., performed in Club Cubic. Other popular clubs include China Rouge in Galaxy Macau, Lion's Bar in MGM Macau, etc.

Source: Macao Government Tourism Office (2017).

The challenges of entertainment tourism

Change in market trend

Today, over 80% of tourists in Macau are from mainland China. In order to modify the products or strategy, one should take the change in visitors' tastes, profiles, and behaviors into account to achieve long-term success. The selection of shows and the provision of different kinds of leisure activities have to be well considered. Repeat visitors would not be interested in the same sets of activities and shows in which they participated in previous visits. In addition, technological advancement should be the biggest concern for businesses which want to be sustainable. The use of the latest technology or the adoption of social media to promote destinations, activities, or shows should be included in the marketing plan.

Image as an entertainment destination

One of the objectives of the Chinese government's 12th Five-Year Plan was to develop Macau as a "World Tourism and Leisure Center", which implied a more family- and leisure-oriented destination. Macau had been considered the "Gaming Capital in Asia" since the last decade. The perception of Macau as a casino city was deep in the heart of tourists. In order to enhance visitors' perceptions and to encourage repeat visitation, an image shift was crucial. The shift of image was difficult, and it had to be done by a carefully designed destination promotional video and marketing communication program. Systematic research must be undertaken to determine the preferred modification in destination image. Successful examples of other countries or regions could be adopted as a reference in planning. For example, the use of the term "integrated resorts" to replace "casino" was adopted commonly in Singapore to diffuse the negative perception of the casino industry. In addition, Las Vegas was a successful example of shifting its image to an entertainment center. Recently, its non-gaming revenue became increasingly important. The CEO of MGM Resorts stated that 75% of Las Vegas's revenue comes from non-gaming activities (Bruno, 2016). These could be used as references for Macau to identify its strength and potential actions.

Seasonality effect

Butler (1994) described seasonality as a temporal imbalance in the phenomenon of tourism. Seasonality could be expressed in terms of certain dimensions, such as numbers of visitors, expenditure of visitors, employment, admission to attractions, and traffic on highways and other forms of transportation. Seasonality is a challenge for destinations. On some days of the year, hotel occupancy could be very high due to holidays, weather, or religious reasons. One example is Golden Week in China. This holiday enables Chinese tourists to travel for a longer period of time, thus leading to the high occupancy rate in hotels and restaurants. Entertainment shows could be seen as a solution and strategy for balancing this irregular flow. The strategy of using entertainment shows is very similar to the concept that some destinations tried to attract MICE business, as this market could generate tourist visitation during low seasons.

Summary

This chapter described the important role of entertainment in the tourism industry and the major entertainment products available in Macau. The entertainment products in Macau can be classified into seven major categories: shows, cultural and creative industries zones, family fun, sports and recreation, beauty and wellness, gaming, and nightlife. This chapter further described the challenges facing the entertainment industry. These challenges include the change of market trend due to the shift of the composition of arriving tourists, the change of destination image, and the seasonality effect.

References

Atlas, R. (1995, May). Sex sells. *Forbes, 155*(10), 49–50.
Banay, S. (2006, March). Hottest casinos. *Forbes*. Retrieved on 02 February 2016, from www.forbes.com/2006/03/22/casinos-travel-gambling-cxsb0323featprint.html
Benston, L. (2003, March). *Park place betting on Dion success*. Retrieved on 03 March 2016, from http://m.lasvegassun.com/news/2003/mar/21/park-place-betting-on-dion-success/
Brueckner, J. K. (1993). Inter-store externalities and space allocation in shopping centers. *The Journal of Real Estate Finance and Economics, 7*(1), 5–16.
Bruno, G. (2016, September 27). *MGM Resorts (MGM) CEO Murren says "75% of the revenue in Las Vegas is non-gaming"*. Retrieved on 21 June 2017, from www.thestreet.com/story/13753231/1/mgm-resorts-mgm-ceo-murren-says-75-of-the-revenue-in-las-vegas-is-non-gaming.html
Butler, R. W. (1994). Seasonality in tourism: Issues and problems. In A. V. Seaton (Ed.), *Tourism: The state of the art* (pp. 332–339). Chichester, UK: Wiley.
Chen, C. K. (2012). Hierarchical linear relationship between the US leisure and entertainment consumption. *Technology in Society, 34*(1), 44–54.
Christiansen, E. M., & Brinkerhoff-Jacobs, J. (1995). Gaming and entertainment: An imperfect union? *The Cornell Hotel and Restaurant Administration Quarterly, 36*(2), 679–694.

Cohen, M. (2011). Macau needs decades to go beyond gambling. *Asia Time Online*. Retrieved on 01 February 2016, from www.atimes.com/atimes/Southeast_Asia/MF30Ae02.html

Guier, C. S. (1999). Broadway shows in spotlight. *Amusement Business, 111*(37), 13.

Heretakis, P. (2008, April). *X + Y = ROI*. Casino Design. Retrieved on 03 March 2017, from http://casinodesignmagazine.com/issue-printer/casino-design-2008-issue International Trade Administration, US Department of Commerce. (2014). *Overseas visitation estimates for U.S. states, cities, and census regions: 2013*. Retrieved on 03 March 2017, from http://tinet.ita.doc.gov/outreachpages/download_data_table/2013_States_and_Cities.pdf

Jones, G. (2009). Hard Rock unveils first phase of expansion in April. *Casino Connection, 5*(4), 17–18, 20.

Kale, S. H. (2006). Designing culturally compatible Internet gaming sites. *UNLV Gaming Research & Review Journal, 10*(1), 41.

Kilby, J., Fox, J., & Lucas, A. F. (2004). *Casino operations management*, 2nd ed. New York: John Wiley.

Leach, R. (2013, March 13). *The Colosseum at Caesars Palace: The $250 million entertainment bet that few believed would succeed*. Retrieved on 01 May 2017, from https://lasvegassun.com/vegasdeluxe/2013/mar/13/colosseum-caesars-palace-250-million-entertainment/

Lucas, A. F., Dunn, W. T., & Kharitonova, A. (2006). Estimating the indirect gaming contribution of bingo rooms. *UNLV Gaming Research & Review Journal, 10*(2), 39.

Lucas, A. F., & Kilby, J. (2008). *Principles of casino marketing*. New York: Okie International.

Lucas, A. F., & Santos, J. (2003). Measuring the effect of casino-operated restaurant volume on slot machine business volume: An exploratory study. *Journal of Hospitality & Tourism Research, 27*(1), 101–117.Macao Government Tourism Office (MGTO). (2017). Retrieved on 03 March 2017, from http://en.macaotourism.gov.mo/index.php

MacDonald, A., & Eadington, W. A. (2008, November). The case for integrated resorts. *Inside Asian Gambling*, 37–43.

Palmeri, C. (2004a). Rebuilding the Roman empire: Can a massive makeover return Caesars to its Old Vegas glory. *Business Week, 3888*, 25–126.

Palmeri, C. (2004b). The $600 million circus maximus. *Business Week, 3912*, 81.

Pine, B. J., & Gilmore, J. H. (1999). *The experience economy: Work is theatre & every business a stage*. Cambridge, MA: Harvard Business Press.

PRLog. (2013, June 5). *Dancing for diversification: Macau.com on Macau's entertainment trends*. Retrieved on 03 March 2017, from www.prlog.org/12150802-dancing-for-diversification-macaucom-on-macaus-entertainment-trends.html

Richards, G. (2001). The experience industry and the creation of attraction. In *Cultural attractions and European tourism* (pp. 55–59). Oxford: CABI Publishing.

Rigby, B. (2008). *Macau gambling growth outstrips Vegas*. Retrieved on 01 May 2017, from www.reuters.com/article/us-travel-leisure-summit-macau-vegas-idUSN1226487020080212

Roehl, W. S. (1996). Competition, casino spending, and use of casino amenities. *Journal of Travel Research, 34*(3), 57–62.

Samuels, J. B. (1999). A qualitative investigation into the characteristics and synergistic relationships of non-gaming recreation/entertainment facilities in casino environments. In *The business of gaming: Economic and management issues, institute for the study of gambling and commercial gaming* (pp. 303–315). Reno, NV: Institute for the Study of Gambling and Commercial Gaming, College of Business Administration, University of Nevada, Reno.

Sternberg, E. (1997). The iconography of the tourism experience. *Annals of Tourism Research, 24*(4), 951–969.

Suh, E. (2006). Estimating the impact of entertainment on the gaming volume of Las Vegas hotel casinos. Doctoral dissertation, University of Nevada, Las Vegas

Suh, E. (2011). Examining the indirect impact of showroom entertainment on hourly slot gaming volume: The case of a Las Vegas hotel-casino. *International Journal of Hospitality Management, 30*(3), 522–529.

Suh, E., & Lucas, A. F. (2011). Estimating the impact of showroom entertainment on the gaming volumes of Las Vegas hotel–casinos. *International Journal of Hospitality Management, 30*(1), 103–111.

Suh, E., & West, J. J. (2010). Estimating the impact of entertainment on the restaurant revenues of a Las Vegas hotel casino: An exploratory study. *International Journal of Hospitality Management, 29*(4), 570–575.

Vora, S. (2007, May). *Las Vegas' most luxurious spots*. Retrieved on 03 March 2017, from www.forbes.com/2007/05/30/vegas-casino-luxury-forbeslife-Forbes

Yoshihashi, P. (1993). Entertainment: Stars fade as Las Vegas bets on families. *Wall Street Journal*, B1.

4 Entertainment tourism management

Evolution of the market

Recently, there were several seismic shifts in the entertainment and media industry. For example, the retirement of Kobe Bryant on 20 November 2015 was announced not only on famous sport channels, but also on major social media channels and Players' Tribune, which provides a digital media focus on athletics. Much traditional media was turning its attention to new, online media. For example, CBS, a traditional TV channel, tried to increase the number of viewers by expanding its business to CBS All Access, a new video-on-demand service. Similarly, Fox began to evaluate channel performance through program viewership, which combined same-day TV ratings and video-on-demand services. At the same time, mobile service providers, such as AT&T and Sprint, provided unlimited data packages as a response to the increasing demand for video streaming. As a result, the most popular gifts in 2015 were streaming video devices and smartphones (Bothun & Vollmer, 2016).

These developments show that the entertainment and media industry was transitioning to deal directly with customers. Despite the content remaining unchanged, the distribution and packages available would be different. In particular, as the technology for both fixed and wireless networks improved drastically and the number of mobile devices, such as tablets and smartphones, available to consumers increased simultaneously, these provided opportunities for the industry to alter its structure, producing methods, distribution channels, and monetization of the content among its landscape. Production and distribution no longer existed only within traditional studios. Hence, people had more choice on what (the content), when (the time), where (the location), and how (the device) to watch. Nowadays, experienced users are attracted by the brands, the experiences, and the platforms of the services providers, which are differentiated by the quality, customization, and convenience of their product.

On one hand, in 2014, despite consumer spending on the audio sector and broadband services increasing 5.5% and 9.2% respectively, it was the smallest increase of the last five years. The represented the audio sector slowing down while the broadband sector was maturing. On the other hand, thanks to the increasing popularity of online and mobile games, video games exhibited a double digit growth in 2014, and the growth rate was expected to accelerate (McKinsey, 2015).

These changes were only part of what was occurring within the entertainment industry. These changes also induced changes in the tourism industry. For example, one of the purposes of a destination developing its brand name is to encourage tourists to visit. Different destinations are focused on different market segments, such as local tourists or international tourists. However, if the destination market does not possess a particular theme, service, feature, or brand, the destination might not be able to achieve the desired outcome. From the tourism perspective, Batchelor (1999) defined destination as a continuum. On one end, destination consisted of a wide range of products, such as theme parks and museums, to encourage tourist visitation. On the other end, destination could be viewed as a country or a group of countries. Therefore, there are cities which market themselves together as tourism regions.

Attraction is a key ingredient of the tourism industry. Visitors not only enjoy the view and facilities of the attraction, but also resolve their mystery of the destination. Broadly speaking, attractions include historic sites, heritage homes, museums, halls of fame, art galleries, botanical gardens, ski hills, aquariums, zoos, water parks, amusement parks, casinos, and cultural attractions.

The recreation and entertainment industry is another fast-growing industry in the world. There are many activities that can be classified as the recreation and entertainment industry. For example, bird watching, fishing, and horse riding are aspects of the recreation and entertainment industry. Golfing, skiing, and diving are other aspects of the industry. These activities require venues of different sizes, and these venues need to hire workers to run amenities, such as gift shops and restaurants. Furthermore, these venues need to manage and promote their facilities.

Consumer behaviors

Nowadays, entertainment and leisure have become one of the main tools for destinations to diversify themselves from other destinations and have become one important driving force for economic revenue. More importantly, the main purpose of traveling for most tourists is to enjoy leisure.

On one hand, according to the content associated with the entertainment, popular entertainment could be classified as follows (Stănciulescu & Jugănaru, 2006):

1 Simple relaxation type of entertainment, such as reading
2 Recreational type of entertainment, such as parks and casinos
3 Cultural type of entertainment, such as museum visiting, language learning
4 Show or performance type of entertainment, such as concerts, musicals, or magic performances
5 Physical health entertainment, such as spas or sports
6 Mental health entertainment, such as piligram or religious tourism
7 Historical type of entertainment, such as visiting a battlefield or memorial
8 Commercial type of entertainment, such as shopping
9 Gastronomic type of entertainment, such as food preparation or production
10 Professional entertainment, such as a field trip or team building
11 Atypical leisure entertainment, such as prestigious entertainment and adventure entertainment

On the other hand, based on the people who are involved, entertainment could be classified as:

1 Social entertainment, which facilitates communication among people
2 Active entertainment, which focuses on physical development, such as sports
3 Creative entertainment, such as drawings or painting
4 Cultural entertainment, which focuses on the discovery of life, environment, and culture
5 Adventure entertainment, which aims at fulfilling the need for excitement, such as skydiving
6 Relaxation entertainment, which aims at releasing stress

Regardless of how entertainment is classified, one important ingredient of entertainment is the entertainer. In the case of magic performances, the magician is the entertainer. In the case of shopping, the sales are the entertainer, and so on. The most important role of the entertainer is to ensure the clients feel acknowledged and valued (Stănciulescu & Jugănaru, 2006).

Furthermore, without a doubt, entertainment creates economic benefits or impacts. Entertainment providers find it important to identify consumer behavior. For example, in the case of a festival, many participants are families. Hence, entertainment providers should understand the entertainment needs of families. In additional, a good marketing manager should realize the decision maker of the family and hence entice that person to join the festivals along with the family. Alternatively, adventure entertainment tends to be popular among singles and younger generations. In order to expand adventure entertainment to married and older generations, marketing managers should address the needs, such as daycare or a children's playground, of these people (Kim, Choi, Agrusa, Wang, & Kim, 2010).

Destination management

According to the changes in the market and consumers of entertainment, tourism destinations should address these changes. The remaining portion of this chapter will use Macau as a specific example to illustrate destination management.

Resource management

Tourism resources

According to information from the Macao Government Tourism Office, there were seven major industries related to entertainment tourism, which were exhibition, cultural creation, family fun, recreational sports, health and spa, gambling, and nightlife. Among these, gambling is one of the most important characteristics of Macau's entertainment tourism. The representatives of gambling in Macau are casinos. The gambling industry in Macau is well developed. There are many mega casinos. When tourists arrive in Macau through border gates or other entry points, they can take shuttles to different casinos. Casinos are open twenty-four hours a day and seven days a week. People under the age of 21 are not allowed to enter. Besides, there are different restaurants in most casinos. Tourists can enjoy delicious foods from different countries. Many shows are located in major casinos. Among all the shows in Macau, the most popular is the House Dancing Water located at the City of Dreams. The show was produced by Franco Dragone, one of the world's greatest showmakers. The production investment exceeded 2 billion HKD. The show was inspired by the "seven emotions" from Confucianism. Combined with various dancing performance, gymnastic artistry, and theater and a main theme of water, this show is one of the most innovative and awe-inspiring productions in the world. Furthermore, there are many excellent cultural creation parks, located in the cultural and creative industrial zone, in Macau. For example, Macau 10 Fantasia was opened in 2008. There are two exhibition halls and 10 exhibition rooms for artistic cultural producers and creative product producers to exhibit their products. Besides, there are regular art classes, activities, and seminars, such as comic parties, cosplay, art exchanges, musicals, and so on. The cultural and creative industrial zone regularly holds art classes such as screenwriting, photoshooting, filming, movies, statues, drawing, and so forth. There are other simple and healthy ways to explore Macau, such as walking along the Coloane Walking Trail, cycling in recreational parks, and so on. Alternatively, people can play golf, go bowling or ice skating, and participate in other water sports. People who prefer excitement can try Coloane Karting Track. Family fun is suitable for all tourists. There are many indoor activities as well as outdoor activities in Macau. People can visit the Macao Science Center and Macau Giant Panda Pavilion for science knowledge and cute pandas. Alternatively, people can visit the beach and recreational parks for healthy recreational activities and family fun. Furthermore, many hotel resorts provide facilities for children, such as children's play rooms. When night falls, Macau, a city that never sleeps, becomes more fascinating. To experience exciting nightlife, people can try bars or ballrooms. Many discos are open until after midnight. Along with many other entertainments, there are many choices for tourists in Macau.

Cultural features

The history of Macau is abundant. Despite traditional Chinese festivals, there are many local festivals, such as the feast of Kun lam, the Feast of the Drunken Dragon, the Procession of Our Lady of Fátima, and so on. In addition to these festivals, there were masses in the church, holy statues tour around the city, and so forth. These activities showed Macau as a fusion of East and West.

Infrastructure resources

Traveling through Macau involves public transportation, particularly public buses. Macau is a city with huge mobile population. The main tools for transportation are public buses. Until August 2015, there were three bus companies in Macau. They were Transmac – Transport Urbanos De Macao, Sociedade de Transportes Colectivos de Macau, and Macau Nova Era de Autocarros Públicos. The three companies together operated 74 different routes. Among the three bus companies, Transmac – Transport Urbanos De Macau had the largest number of buses, and it was the only one that obtained ISO certification. All bus companies reduced energy consumption and their emissions to implement green transportation. The main power sources of most buses are mixed power and natural gas. The common problems of public buses in Macau are bad service attitude, missing stops, and speeding.

Industrial management

There are rules and regulations in each industry, including the entertainment industry in Macau. To prevent illegal gambling activities, the Macau government established the Gaming Inspection and Coordination Bureau (GICB). The objective of GICB includes, but is not limited to, providing advice and assistance to the chief executive of Macau of the operation of casinos or other forms of gambling; providing and executing gambling policies; and supervising and monitoring the financial and business activities of gambling operators.

Understanding and regulating tourists

Until February 2017, 2,495,196 tourists had arrived in Macau. Tourists from mainland China represented the biggest proportion (up to 66.7%), followed by Hong Kong, Taiwan, South Korea, and Japan. Among tourists from mainland China, most were from Guangdong Province. There were over 780,000 tourists in a single month, which represented 46.8% of the total number of Chinese tourists arrived Macau in 2017.

To regulate tourists arriving in Macau, the Macau government put tourists' reminders on public transportation and notice boards on all major tourists' attractions. Since there are many tourists to Macau, the quality varies. Therefore, the major entry points of Macau have become the area for tourists management. The Public Security Policy Force is the main regulating authority. The Public Security Policy Force is responsible for many duties, such as maintaining public order, preventing and investigating crime, protecting public interests and properties, and so on. Responsibilities related to tourists' regulations include issuing visas, permits, or other corresponding documents and executing immigration policies.

In the future, simple tourist attractions likely would not be able to attract tourists anymore. More tourist attractions, such as Happy Valley in Shenzhen and OCT East, are adding entertainment characteristics. To increase the competitiveness of Macau's tourism, entertainment products should be enhanced. Nowadays, business travel and sightseeing tours are moving toward integrated travel. The entertainment industry in Macau is expanding. It evolved from an industry solely based on gambling to an industry with multiple entertainment items. In the future, Macau should strive to protect its existing resources and provide entertainment products targeting a wide range of tourists. For example, several interesting local events could be combined into one event. This would not only increase its popularity among the world, but also package the festival with charisma and entertaining features. The Macau Grand Prix is a successful example, as the Food Festival was usually held during the same period. Furthermore, public transportation options, particularly buses, in Macau should improve their service quality. The light rail transit was expected to be finished soon, which would reduce the pressure to existing public transportation.

Summary

This chapter discussed the evolution of entertainment in the last decade. With the increasing popularity of mobile services, people have changed the time, location, and methods used to obtain entertainment services. Hence, it is important for entertainment providers to understand consumer behavior and manage their resources carefully. This chapter further discussed different destination management concerns using Macau as a specific example.

References

Batchelor, R. (1999). Strategic marketing of tourism destinations. In *The international marketing of travel and tourism* (pp. 181–195). London: Macmillan Education.
Bothun, D., & Vollmer, C. (2016). *2016 entertainment & media industry trends*. Retrieved on 01 May 2017, from www.strategyand.pwc.com/trends/2016-entertainment-media-industry-trends
Kim, S. S., Choi, S., Agrusa, J., Wang, K. C., & Kim, Y. (2010). The role of family decision makers in festival tourism. *International Journal of Hospitality Management, 29*(2), 308–318.
McKinsey. (2015). *Global media report 2015*. Retrieved on 01 May 2017, from www.mckinsey.com/~/media/McKinsey/dotcom/client_service/Media%20and%20Entertainment/PDFs/McKinsey%20Global%20Report%202015_UK_October_2015.ashx
Stănciulescu, G., & Jugănaru, I. D. (2006). *Entertainment and entertainer in tourism*. Bucharest: Uranus Publishing House.

5   Trends of entertainment tourism

Virtual reality application in entertainment tourism

To enhance destination experiences for visitors, destination marketing managers have explored new information and communication technologies to promote the destination (Agapito & Lacerda, 2014). For example, one of the most popular games in 2016, Pokémon Go (Gesenhues, 2016), employs augmented reality to enhance players' experience. Specifically, this game uses GPS and mobile device cameras to created augmented reality. Furthermore, hotels, shops, and even destinations use this game to entice people to visit the area. This is an excellent example of using new technologies to promote a destination.

Virtual reality has been recognized as new generation Internet and computer platform. Virtual reality, when combined with tourism, could not only produce a new tourism experience and change tourism patterns, but also could revolutionize people's recognition of tourism. This technology is an important area for development for future travel, tours, and cultural exhibitions. The rise of virtual reality is going to break the traditional pattern of sales in tourism and provide revolutionary changes. Besides, businesses can use this new technology to increase service quality. Compared with traditional sales methods, such as pictures and plain descriptions, virtual reality allows tourists to experience the product prior to arrival and speed up their decision process. Therefore, many businesses value highly the application of virtual reality in entertainment tourism.

Rise of virtual reality in entertainment tourism in Macau

Combine virtual reality and entertainment tourism

Through virtual reality in entertainment tourism in Macau, tourists could see not only the details of entertainment tourism in Macau, but also tourism resources that are not open or are not regularly open to public. Tourists could obtain first-hand information and characteristics of entertainment tourism in Macau. Furthermore, tourists could virtually visit the precise destinations they were interested in, and they could choose the appropriate destinations to visit. Virtual reality application in entertainment tourism could effectively assist decision making for tourists, demonstrate experience before play, and allow tourists to customize their routes and activities in Macau.

Due to the characteristics of virtual reality, virtual reality in entertainment tourism has helped tourists experience tourism and the unique charisma of entertainment tourism in Macau. Travel operators provide virtual reality entertainment tourism experiences and entertainment projects. In addition, virtual reality has allowed tourists to recover the route they have tried. Therefore, this could provide a more direct option for tourists to decide their travel route. Furthermore, travel operators could learn more about the preference of individuals and provide more appropriate tourism products.

The most common application of virtual reality is tourist attractions or theme parks. Most theme parks integrate the theme park with virtual reality and entertainment projects, such as an offline virtual reality experience, Virtual Engineering Center (VEC), and VR Theme Park. The objective is to increase participation and interaction with tourists and attract more customers via the innovative virtual reality project. Through the combination of virtual reality and entertainment tourists, Macau needed to infiltrate tourists' minds via visual presentation and audio sounds, with the objective to create strong leisure motives and projects that were attractive.

The business mode of virtual reality in entertainment tourism

Many virtual reality equipment providers and platforms hosted the content. Unfortunately, the content involved was relatively weak, especially content related to entertainment tourism in Macau and the content combination with virtual reality. Therefore, it would be profitable for the content producers to create content related to entertainment tourism in Macau.

Content providers could provide immersive entertainment experiences in Macau to tourists. Furthermore, content providers could interact with major travel agents to provide a full package service combining creation, publishing, and promotion services. In mainland China, major virtual reality content providers are travel agents and tourist attractions businesses.

The issues of entertainment tourism in Macau

Bright future of tourism development in Macau

Due to the financial distress in the world, Macau had been repositioning and adjusting since 2014. In particular, the future development of the gambling industry, which was the main component of the entertainment industry in

Macau, is not optimistic. The growth rate has been negative in certain years. However, in the long run, the entertainment industry in Macau has shown a long-term growing trend. The entertainment industry continues to be the driving force of economic growth and has maintained a strategic position in the national economy of Macau.

From the national perspective, first, China entered into an era where the mass public could enjoy leisure. China was entering into a new developmental phase. The focus switched from public tours to mixed-composite travel. The proportion of leisure expenditure and leisure time with respect to total consumption continued to increase. Travel, leisure, and entertainment became highlights of people's lives. Entertainment tourism represented a relatively big proportion of Macau's economic structure. Major entertainment brands, such as Lisboa Casino, the Venetian, the Galaxy Resort, the Sands, and the Fisherman's Wharf, had strong international influences. The image of an international entertainment tourists' center was well recognized. Furthermore, there were an increasing number of investments in mega entertainment projects and entertainment complexes. The entertainment tourism business was a strong driving force for economic development in Macau.

Second, since one of the objectives of the Chinese government was to develop Macau sustainably, there were many policy supports associated. According to the 13th Five-Year Plan from the State Council, the Chinese government was going to 1) enhance cooperation in tourism between Hong Kong, Macau, and Taiwan, 2) support tourism development in Hong Kong and Macau, 3) enhance communication with the tourism industry in Taiwan, and 4) provide structures and orders to tourism in Hong Kong, Macau, and Taiwan. The main objective was to make Hong Kong, Macau, Zhuhai, and several cities in China become the main attractions to international tourists and to develop Macau into a "World Center of Tourism and Leisure".

Finally, the synergetic effects between Hong Kong, Macau, and Guangzhou successfully enhanced the economy of Macau. The Free Trade Area (FTA) in Guangdong provided policy support to integrate tourism between Hong Kong, Macau, and Guangdong. The integration agreement included the co-development of tourism products, tourism resources, tourism markets, transportation construction, infrastructure, and information system. Furthermore, the integration agreement enhanced communication on tourism policy, system and management and integration among tourism talents, technology, and capital. These cooperative agreements effectively increased the potential development of entertainment tourism in Macau.

From the international perspective, the national policy, "One belt one road", also provided unprecedented opportunities to develop entertainment tourism in Macau. In particular, with the aim of "World Center of Tourism and Leisure" and the support of the government, Macau could develop "sea tourism" with countries such as India and several Africa nations, and so on, along the Europe-Asia maritime trade route. Macau could project the image of "World Center of Tourism and Leisure" to more countries around the world. This provided immeasurable meaning to enhance the competitiveness of Macau's entertainment tourism in the world.

Diversified development of entertainment tourism business

Nowadays, leisure and entertainment economy have become an unstoppable mainstream. Their increasing popularity and diversified consumer demand have provided new opportunities to entertainment tourism in Macau. Besides, the diversification of Macau's economy depended on the diversification of sources markets and tourism products. Recently, as the international economy slowed down, the traditional gambling industry has slowed down simultaneously. To change the one-dimensional image of a city of gambling, tourism in Macau has moved towards an integrated leisure and entertainment complex. The leading hotels are high-end hotels, such as Wynn's Palace and Parisian. These hotels did not increase their focus on gambling; instead, they tried to consider the demand and needs of consumers from different categories. These actions were merely micro – restructuring among businesses. Furthermore, the Macau government wanted to nurture cultural and exhibition tourism as the new driving forces for the transformation of Macau's tourism. The objective was to create a development framework integrating gambling, exhibition, culture, health, shopping, leisure, creative culture, and business. Although the effect of the transformations remains to be seen, one would expect the future of entertainment tourism in Macau to be more diversified.

Stratification of entertainment tourism products

The enhancement, refinement, and stratification of tourism products in Macau depends heavily on the adjustment and stratification of the source market. Besides, as the leisure entertainment market has become more prosperous among the public, the transformation of the source market induced new demand for diversifications. Therefore, to maintain the competitiveness of the industry, the entertainment tourism industry in Macau needed to adjust their products' position and strategies according to the new environment. The stratification of the entertainment tourism product came from two sides. The first stratification came from creative innovation. This stratification could be initiated by internal adjustments according to the core system. Alternatively, it could be initiated by situations from the newly developed markets. The new series of theme parks and spa leisure complexes are examples induced by the newly developed markets. These new products increased the number of choices available. The second stratification came from the classification of product quality. There were two steps to this stratification. The first step involved people professionally examining existing products, which were mainly targeting the high-end market. The second step involved people re-classifying and re-distributing the products to the public market, the family market, and the youth market according to market conditions. In conclusion, entertainment tourism in Macau is going to experience a massive revolution in business format, markets, and tourism form and will exhibit the characteristics of popularization, socialization, leisure, and diversification.

Adaptation of new technologies to entertainment tourism

Recently, many new technologies, such as virtual reality, enhanced reality, mixed reality, and so on, have been used widely to enhance the quality, novelty, and experience of entertainment tourism. Among these new technologies, the most popularly applied is virtual reality. Virtual reality is a technology that creates a simulated environment using a computer. It allows people to experience and interact with a three-dimensional world. It creates an indistinguishably real and believable experience and makes people fall into the environment. The use of virtual reality is expected to be the new trend for entertainment tourism products in Macau. The technology allows people to experience St Paul's Ruins while the corresponding history of St Paul's Ruin is beside the screen (Moura, 2016).

Although Macau applied virtual reality (VR) on sales and experience exhibitions, the problem in the future is how to create massive high-quality virtual reality in tourism products. This increased the level of information of Macau tourism in general and demonstrated most of the tourism resources in Macau through online platforms. Tourists could experience entertainment products in Macau through VR devices and familiarize themselves with entertainment tourism in Macau.

Until now, the cost of producing virtual reality content was relatively high, which made the cost difficult to average out among tourists. However, this technology could be applied easily to high-end customers or tourism real estate, which was a branch of real estate business targeting tourists or non-local people as potential buyers. Since one of the characteristics of high-end entertainment tourism products was high price and high profit margins, the cost to users was high and the sales were difficult to complete. The presence of virtual reality allowed these customers to pre-experience the destination before making their decision, which increased the likelihood of completing sales. Furthermore, due to the high price and high profit margin, the cost of producing virtual reality contents could be shared among sales easily. Therefore, virtual reality could be applied to this niche market widely.

Tourists could enhance their experience of interactive entertainment through VR technology and system upgrade of entertainment tourism facilities in Macau. In the future, tourists in the real tourist attraction, through the VR devices, could interact and communicate with people who were experiencing the attraction through virtual reality. People from different places could meet in the same "place". The ultimate goal is to connect from real to virtual and vice versa and enhance the experience of entertainment tourism in Macau.

Summary

This chapter described the new technology impact on entertainment tourism and discussed the trend in Macau entertainment tourism development. The tourism department in Macau could apply VR technology to different entertainment tourism institutions and tourist attractions in the future. Since VR allows tourists to preview the destination, plan their route, experience certain attractions, and increase information exchange, it helps tourists determine their plan and schedule of entertainment tourism in Macau. Furthermore, VR users could experience the attractions with others who were located in the destination and vice versa. This would increase the attractiveness and competitiveness of Macau. The existence of virtual reality would revolutionize and change the traditional sales method of entertainment tourism in Macau. There are many possibilities between VR and tourism. Despite the high cost of production, immature technologies, small market size, and low recognition, as technologies and equipment improve, without any doubt, entertainment tourism in Macau will adapt VR technologies more frequently in the future.

References

Agapito, D., & Lacerda, A. (2014). Marketing and brand design of destination experiences: The role of ICT. *Journal of Spatial and Organizational Dynamics, 2*(3), 201–216.

Gesenhues, A. (2016, December 14). *Google's top searches in 2016: Pokémon Go & iPhone 7 outrank Donald Trump, Prince & Powerball*. Retrieved on 01 May 2017, from http://searchengineland.com/googles-top-searches-2016-pokemon-go-iphone-7-outrank-donald-trump-prince-powerball-265476

Moura, N. (2016, April 06). *Macau through VR goggles*. Retrieved on 01 May 2017, from http://macaubusinessdaily.com/Business/Macau-through-VR-goggles

6 Entertainment product evaluation

A case of tourist experience in Macau

Introduction

The tourism and entertainment industry is an important component in the world's service sector. International tourists increased from 20 million in 1950 to over 1 billion in 2015. Moreover, for any 11 employees, 1 employee is working in the tourism industry; 29% of exported services come from international travel (UNWTO, 2016). Bond (2013) reported that the revenue from the entertainment industry in 2013 was USD 1.639 trillion and estimated revenue was going to increase to USD 2.152 trillion in 2017. Asia, particularly China, has experienced a huge growth in the nightlife and entertainment industry. The number of nightclubs, bars, karaoke clubs, and discos reached 200,000 in 2013. The revenue generated reached 44.8 billion Renminbi in the same year. Similar patterns were also observed in many Southeast Asian countries (Global Gaming Expo Asia, 2015).

Entertainment tourism has received more attention, not only from practitioners, but also from academics (Adeboye, 2012). Tourists enjoy traveling around the world to experience different entertainment products, such as concerts, magic performances, dance performances, and talk shows. Hughes (2000) stated that entertainment activities are a type of art performance, while Xu (2010) defined entertainment activities as tourism products that provide memorable experiences. Entertainment products, particularly gambling, not only provide fun to tourists, but also increase the attractiveness of the destinations (Loi & Pearce, 2012). Gambling has become more important in driving economic growth in many countries such as Singapore, the United States, Australia, and throughout Europe (McCarthy, 2002).

The entertainment industry consists of a wide range of activities including recreational activities, such as fishing and bird watching; sports activities, such as horse riding and golfing; and educational visits, such as visiting entertaining stops. All these activities require a large staff to manage, maintain, and operate the site. This industry is expected to be one of the fastest-growing sectors. The growth of employment from this industry was around

2.1% per annum (Hospitality Industry Education Advisory Committee, 2016).

Macau liberalized the gambling industry in 2002. The local government and the Chinese government have been encouraging Macau to diversify its focus on gambling and have been promoting Macau to be the "World Centre of Tourism and Leisure", which was also part of the 12th Five-Year Plan in China (Macao Government Tourism Office, 2016a). Furthermore, Guangdong and Macau recently signed the "Guangdong-Macau Cooperation Framework Agreement". The agreement aimed at transforming Macau to a more family- and business-oriented travel destination.

The total number of tourists who arrived Macau in 2015 was over 28 million, a 0.3% increase relative to the prior year. The proportion of tourists from China, Hong Kong, and Taiwan was 60.2%, 25.2%, and 2.8% respectively. The revenue generated from the gambling industry was over USD 300 billion, which represented around 90% of the GDP of Macau in 2015. The GDP per capita of Macau was also one of the highest in Asia (DSEC, 2016a). Given the dominance of gambling in Macau, it would be difficult to expect a huge diversification, regardless whether in terms of revenue sources or new attractions, in the near future.

Macau surpassed Las Vegas, in terms of gaming revenue and in terms of destination ranking, many years ago. However, challenges from other nearby destinations, such as Singapore, the Philippines, South Korea, and Taiwan, have remained (Blanke & Chiesa, 2013). The entertainment industry is composed of many entities, such as media, Internet, and computer games. However, since these do not necessarily involve traveling, they are not part of the tourism industry. Few studies have focused on entertainment products in the tourism sector. This study tried to investigate the importance and performance of the entertainment products in Macau from the customers' perspective. The specific objectives of this study were as follows:

1 To review the historical development of entertainment in Macau
2 To evaluate entertainment product performance for tourists' experience
3 To provide suggestions and recommendations for firms' strategic management of service encounters

Literature review

Historical development of the entertainment industry in Macau

After liberalizing the gambling industry a decade ago, diversification from the gambling industry became the top priority for both the local Macau government and the Chinese government. Several attempts tried to diverge from the gambling industry. In 2008, Cirque du Soleil, a Canadian entertainment company and the largest theatrical producer in the world, launched ZAiA in Venetian Macau (Cirque du Soleil, 2016). Similar to many other successful shows in Las Vegas, such as KA in MGM Grand, O in Bellagio, and Mystère in Treasure Island, ZAiA was a resident show, which meant the show performed regularly in the same location, and ZAiA was the only resident show in Asia. However, due to various issues, possibly competition from another similar show, the House of Dancing Water, and low audience numbers, ZAiA was terminated in 2012. The House of Dancing Water show, a show that combined dancing and circus performance, has been considered a recent success (Melco Crown, 2016). Various other entertainments, such as Taboo at City of Dreams, splash pool parties at Hard Rock Hotel, and the China Rouge nightclub at Galaxy, were also developed. Furthermore, Galaxy Waldo, the first entertainment project of Galaxy in Macau, opened in 2004. The potential of the entertainment industry in Macau was enormous and moved the tourism and entertainment to a sustainable development (Galaxy, 2004). In Macau, the number of entertainment businesses increased from 68 in 2001 to over 300 in 2015 (DSEC, 2016b; see Figure 6.1).

These entertainment businesses also benefited Macau in other ways. For example, people who purchased some entertainment products, such as shows, usually pre-ordered 1–2 months ahead. This was quite different from the usual impulse purchases reported in many

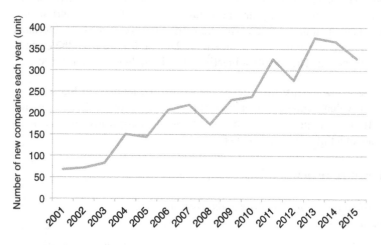

Figure 6.1 New entertainment company statistics in Macau
Source: DSEC (2016b).

studies. This indicated that people were worried about whether they could get show tickets. The average transaction was around 2,500 HKD with a minimum stay of two nights. The composition of visitors included tourists from Hong Kong, Taiwan, South Korea, China, and Singapore (PRLog, 2013). Despite this success in terms of audience and the associated benefits, the revenue generated was minimal relative to gaming revenue. Furthermore, combined with the failure of ZAiA, this might explain why there were not many similar performance launches in Macau (Cohen, 2011).

Tourism and entertainment products

The word "entertainment" came from "entertain". The original meaning was to enjoy life and get going. A more philosophical meaning of entertainment can be found in Besciu (2013). According to the authors, entertainment means "to inspire, to give meaning and interest to life in the community, to create a certain climate, dynamism, in an accommodation and food unit". From a tourism perspective, entertainment is mainly about the creation of good feelings. This might include sports or games, which were free to participate in and in which mutual contacts were possible, or shows or concerts, which were not free and contained minimal interactive contacts. The related concept is leisure, which is also one of the motivations for traveling. Leisure concerns the relaxation and comfort of the passengers and entertainment within the sites. Entertainment leisure is one of the methods to differentiate different destinations and is an important source of income.

Due to the increasing popularity of entertainment tourism and its contribution to the development of tourism (Adeboye, 2012), many tourism researchers have attempted to understand tourism and entertainment products. Murphy (1985) treated destinations as one of the tourism products, and the author used demand and supply analysis to understand the consumption characteristics. Gunn (1988) defined tourism products as a combination of the consumption experience on various travel services, such as information, transportation, accommodation, and attractions, during tourists' stay on the site. Travel services and the inputs from the destination created experiences for visitors (Smith, 1994). Robinson, Lück, Smith, and Lackey (2013) included tourist attractions as part of the tourism products. The author claimed that tourist attractions are the most important. "Without attractions, there would be no need for other tourism services. Indeed, tourism as such would not exist if it were not for attractions". At the same time, in many scenarios, tourist attractions and entertainment are inseparable. For example, areas for people to participate (sport stadium), listen (concert hall), and watch (theaters and museums) are entertainment venues. These are not only tourist attractions, but also entertainment sites. Another example is Las Vegas. Las Vegas is not only famous for casinos, but is also famous for the numerous numbers of live shows available (Hughes & Benn, 1997). Nowadays, the business has evolved to provide virtual reality experiences for people.

Broadly speaking, entertainment includes a wide range of activities, such as concerts, shows, street performances, festivals, and so on. Besciu (2013) defined entertainment as activities such as watching movies and sport competitions, dancing, and visiting theme parks. According to Besciu (2013), the popularity of entertainments should depend on the content of the activities. Show entertainment was the most popular, followed by cultural entertainment and entertainment to maintain physical fitness. Alternatively, Chen (2012) defined entertainment as a type of popular performing arts with the aim to provide a memorable and pleasurable experience. Xu (2010) provided a similar definition as Chen (2012), but the author included entertainment as part of the tourism product.

In Macau, numerous resorts offer entertainment on an international level. The nightlife in Macau is diverse and exciting. Based on the definition of the Macau government, entertainment products include shows, cultural and creative industry, family fun, sports and recreation, beauty and wellness, gaming, and nightlife. Among these classifications, the most popular activities other than gaming are the Macau Tower Skyjump and related activities, such as Sky watch. Other non-gaming activities include a "Gangnam Style" concert from PSY, clubbing events at Club Cubic and the China Rouge nightclub at Galaxy Macau, Taboo at City of Dreams, and splash pool parties at Hard Rock Hotel Macau (PRLog, 2013).

Importance–Performance Analysis (IPA)

The original use of IPA as an analytical tool for evaluating consumer ratings dates back to 25 years ago (Pritchard & Havitz, 2006). The use of IPA consists of a simple diagram. Usually, the X-axis provides the scores of performance, while the Y-axis shows the scores of importance. A cross located in the diagram divides it into four quadrants. The first quadrant is the "Concentrate Here" quadrant. This quadrant reflects performance of the products which is felt to be behind, but is important to the customers. The second quadrant is the "Keep Up the Good Work" quadrant. This quadrant reflects that the product is important to customers and that the performance met the requirement. The third quadrant is the "Low Priority" quadrant. This quadrant shows that the customers do not place much value on this product while the performance of the product is not

Quadrant I **Concentrate Here** High Importance–Low Performance	**Quadrant II** **Keep Up the Good Work** High Importance–High Performance
Quadrant III **Low Priority** Low Importance–Low Performance	**Quadrant IV** **Possible Overkill** Low Importance–High Performance

IMPORTANCE (vertical label on left)

PERFORMANCE

Figure 6.2 Importance–Performance Analysis grid
Source: Martilla and James (1977).

satisfying either. The final quadrant is the "Possible Overkill" quadrant. This quadrant shows that customers do not place much value on this product but that the performance of the product is above what the consumer wants (see Figure 6.2).

IPA is a useful method to identify the strengths, weaknesses, and areas of improvement of products, service attributes, or strategies (Martilla & James, 1977; Matzler, Bailom, Hinterhuber, Renzl, & Pichler, 2004; Linda & To, 2010). Many researchers use this method to investigate consumer satisfaction and to pinpoint areas of improvement and develop planning strategies (Wu & Shieh, 2009, 2010; Yavas & Shemwell, 2001). Numerous tourism and hospitality researchers have applied IPA to study the discrepancy between consumer satisfaction and importance (Zhang & Chow, 2004; Deng, 2007; Tonge & Moore, 2007; Chang & Yang, 2008; Frauman & Banks, 2011). Pritchard and Havitz (2006) applied IPA to study the attributes of a destination. O'Leary and Deegan (2005) used attributes, such as nightlife, culture, history, environment, and so forth, to study the perception of tourists prior to visit and after the visit. Joppe, Martin, & Waalen (2001) studied the perception of tourists on products and services using IPA and provided recommendations on the corresponding strength and weakness. Sorensson and Friedrichs (2013) studied the perception of tourists on environment and sustainability of the destination. The results were used to provide recommendations for future improvements. Hansen and Bush (1999) exerted the simplicity and effectiveness of using IPA to identify areas of improvement and develop marketing strategies for researchers and practitioners.

Methodology

Research instruments

A self-administered questionnaire was created from information obtained from a literature review. The questionnaire was reviewed by three panel experts. One of the panel experts was senior vice president of Galaxy Entertainment Group, one was an academic involved in tourism study, and one was a senior manager of SJM Holdings Limited. The composition of the panel experts was intended to represent a sufficient perspective from the industry. The resultant questionnaire was sent for pilot testing with a group of 25 tourists for efficacy and clarity. Revisions to the questionnaire were made based on the recommendations of the respondents. The final instrument contained three sections. The first section collected respondent demographic information. The second section identified the characteristics of entertainment activities. The last section measured the importance–performance of the entertainment, including shows, cultural and creative industry, family fun, sports and recreation, beauty and wellness, gaming, and nightlife (MGTO, 2016b). Each of these entertainment experiences was further classified into several activities. Table 6.1 lists all the entertainment experiences and the corresponding activities in each item. The evaluation of importance and performance is ranked from 1 to 5 based on the Likert scale, with 1 = not important, 2 = least important, 3 = neutral, 4 = important, and 5 = very important. The decision to use a five-point scale instead of a seven-point scale was to reduce respondent frustration and to improve the accuracy of the responses (Shifflet, 1992). The questionnaire was prepared in two languages: English and Chinese.

Table 6.1 Entertainment products in Macau

Categories	*Products*
Shows	Popular concerts; classical concerts; magic performances; theater shows
Cultural and creative	Street entertainment; local arts community
Family fun	Museums; themed shopping; themed dining
Sports and recreation	Spectator sports; golf; horse riding
Beauty and wellness	Medical beauty care; spas
Gaming	Horse racing; greyhound racing; lottery; casino
Nightlife	Bars and lounges; dance clubs

Source: MGTO (2016b).

Data collection

The research was conducted in three major tourist departure points in Macau, which were the Border Gate, Macau International Airport, and the Outer Harbour Ferry Terminal, during the months of November and December 2016. These data collection locations were chosen because these are the three main channels for tourists to arrive and depart Macau (Macao Government Public Security Police Force Headquarters [FSM], 2016). This study employed convenience sampling to collect data. In total, 400 questionnaires were distributed at the departure points, and 308 usable questionnaires were obtained. The average time spent in filling out the questionnaire was 10 minutes.

Results and discussion

Profile of respondents

A total of 400 questionnaires were distributed to respondents, and 308 usable questionnaires were collected, a response rate of 77%. The demographic profile of the respondents is presented in Table 6.2. There were 221 (71.8%) respondents from mainland China, followed by Hong Kong (20.5%), Taiwan (2.9%), South Korea (1.9%), and Japan (1.3%). Other respondents were from the United States and Australia. There were 182 (59.1%) females and 126 (40.9%) males among the respondents. The main age group was 25–35 (35.4%), followed by 16–25 (24.7%), 36–45 (20.5%), 46–55 (15.9%), 56–65 (2.9%), and over 65 (0.6%). Within these age groups, the highest satisfaction level was the 36–45 age group and the lowest was the over 65 age group. There were 48.7% respondents with a university education, 35.4% with high school or below, 8.8% with diploma, and 7.1% with masters or above. Within these education groups, the highest satisfaction level was diploma and the lowest was high school or below. There were 32.5% respondents with sub-professional careers, followed by student (19.2%), self-employed (12.3%), professional (10.1%), blue collar (10.1%), unemployed (7.5%), housewife (7.1%), and retired (1.3%). Within these occupation groups, the highest satisfaction level was the self-employed group and the lowest was the unemployed group. Most of the respondents had monthly income of less than USD 10,000. The satisfaction level across different occupations, different education levels, and different age groups was roughly the same. Furthermore, most of the respondents came to Macau for holiday or leisure. Within different purposes, people who came to Macau for transit had the highest

Table 6.2 The demographic profile of respondents

		Frequency (N = 308)	%	Satisfaction		F/t	LSD
				Mean	SD		
Country of origin	Mainland China	221	71.8	3.40	0.37	2.07	
	Hong Kong	63	20.5	3.27	0.24		
	Taiwan	9	2.9	3.51	0.22		
	South Korea	6	1.9	3.33	0.12		
	Japan	4	1.3	3.57	0.49		
	Other	5	1.6	3.34	0.22		
Gender	Male	126	40.9	3.38	0.30	0.06	
	Female	182	59.1	3.37	0.37		
Age	16–25	76	24.7	3.39	0.42	2.85**	3 > 1, 2, 4, 5, 6
	25–35	109	35.4	3.38	0.33		
	36–45	63	20.5	3.47	0.31		
	46–55	49	15.9	3.28	0.25		
	56–65	9	2.9	3.17	0.10		
	65+	2	0.6	3.07	0.51		
Education	High school or below	109	35.4	3.32	0.29	3.18**	2 > 4, 3, 1
	Diploma	27	8.8	3.53	0.53		
	University degree	150	48.7	3.39	0.32		
	Masters or above	22	7.1	3.43	0.41		

Variable	Category	n	%	Mean	SD	F	Post-hoc
Occupation	Self-employed (e.g., businessman)	38	12.3	3.48	0.37	2.42**	1 > 6, 7, 2, 3, 8, 4, 5
	Housewife	22	7.1	3.39	0.32		
	Student	59	19.2	3.33	0.30		
	Retired	4	1.3	3.25	0.07		
	Unemployed	23	7.5	3.19	0.29		
	Professional (e.g., doctor, lawyer)	31	10.1	3.42	0.40		
	Sub-professional (e.g., clerical officer)	100	32.5	3.42	0.36		
	Blue collar (e.g., worker)	31	10.1	3.30	0.28		
Annual Income	USD 10,000 or less	123	39.9	3.33	0.33	1.46	
	USD 10,001–20,000	118	38.3	3.42	0.38		
	USD 20,001–30,000	51	16.6	3.40	0.25		
	USD 30,0001–40,000	8	2.6	3.48	0.38		
	USD 40,0001 or above	8	2.6	3.25	0.32		
Purpose	Holiday/leisure	200	64.9	3.40	0.36	4.44**	4 > 1, 3, 5, 2
	Business/convention and exhibition	11	3.6	3.27	0.22		
	Visiting friends and relatives	79	25.6	3.34	0.25		
	Transit	2	0.6	4.29	1.01		
	Other	16	5.2	3.33	0.39		
Stay	Less than 1 day	126	40.9	3.32	0.34	3.93**	2 > 3, 1
	1–2 days	159	51.6	3.43	0.30		
	3 days or more	23	7.5	3.38	0.52		
Frequency	First time	62	20.1	3.41	0.38	0.76	
	Repeat	246	79.9	3.37	0.33		
Spent on entertainment	USD 100 or less	126	40.9	3.30	0.29	3.20**	4 > 3, 2, 5, 1
	USD 101–1,000	141	45.8	3.43	0.34		
	USD 1,001–2,000	28	9.1	3.45	0.43		
	USD 2,001–3,000	5	1.6	3.51	0.59		
	USD 3,001 or above	8	2.6	3.41	0.34		

**$p < 0.05$.

level of satisfaction. Over 79.9% of the respondents were repeat visitors. In addition, 86% of the respondents spent less than USD 1,000 on entertainment.

The characteristics of tourists' entertainment behavior in Macau

Table 6.3 shows the entertainment products visitors experienced. The total number of products experienced was 868. This means that, on average, each respondent experienced 2.82 tourism products. The most popular product was themed shopping. Casino was the second, and magic performances was the third. The top three products represented over 60% of the total product experienced. The last 10 products only represented less than 10% of the total product experienced. Based on the classification in Table 6.1, Table 6.4 shows the number of tourists who experienced the products within the category. Given that family fun included themed shopping and themed dining, it was the category that most of the respondents experienced. The gaming category included casino, horse racing, greyhound racing, and lottery.

Table 6.3 Total number of entertainment product items experienced by tourists (N = 308)

Entertainment Items	Sum	SD	Rank
Themed shopping	215	0.46	1
Casino	189	0.49	2
Magic performances	141	0.50	3
Themed dining	81	0.44	4
Local arts community	75	0.43	5
Museums	41	0.34	6
Bars and lounges	32	0.31	7
Spas	23	0.26	8
Theaters	12	0.19	9
Popular concerts	10	0.18	10
Spectator sports	9	0.17	11
Street entertainment	9	0.17	12
Classical concerts	8	0.16	13
Greyhound racing	5	0.13	14
Dance clubs	4	0.11	15
Horse riding	4	0.11	16
Lottery	3	0.10	17
Medical beauty care	3	0.10	18
Horse racing	2	0.08	19
Golf	2	0.08	20

Table 6.4 Total number of entertainment product categories experienced by tourists (N = 308)

Entertainment Product Categories	Total	SD	Rank
Family fun	337	0.75	1
Gaming	199	0.53	2
Shows	171	0.55	3
Cultural and creative	84	0.47	4
Nightlife	36	0.32	5
Beauty and wellness	26	0.28	6
Sports and recreation	15	0.24	7

Table 6.5 Mean scores of entertainment products in importance and performance (satisfaction) (N = 308)

Entertainment Products/Dimensions	Important		Performance (Satisfaction)		Gaps
	Mean	Rank	Mean	Rank	
Shows	3.51	3	3.67	2	−0.16
Cultural and creative	3.26	4	3.37	3	−0.09
Family fun	3.89	1	3.88	1	0.08
Sports and recreation	2.97	6	3.05	7	−0.42
Beauty and wellness	2.95	7	3.10	6	−0.13
Gaming	3.52	2	3.37	4	0.15
Nightlife	3.16	5	3.20	5	−0.04

However, around 95% of the respondents who participated in gaming actually visited casinos only. Only 5% of the respondents participated in other gaming activities, such as horse racing or greyhound racing.

Figure 6.3 shows the IPA for entertainment products in Macau. The mean scores were used as mid-point for the X- and Y-axes. One dimension was located in the Concentrate Here quadrant, two dimensions were located in the Keep Up the Good Work quadrant, and four dimensions were located in the Low Priority quadrant. No dimension fell into the Possible Overkill quadrant. This means the entertainment products provided by the Macau tourism industry fulfilled most of the needs of tourists. The dimensions in the Low Priority region mean the tourists do not place much value on the products and the performance of the products is bad, while the dimensions in the Keep Up the Good Work region mean the tourists value the products and the performance of the products is sufficient to meet the need of

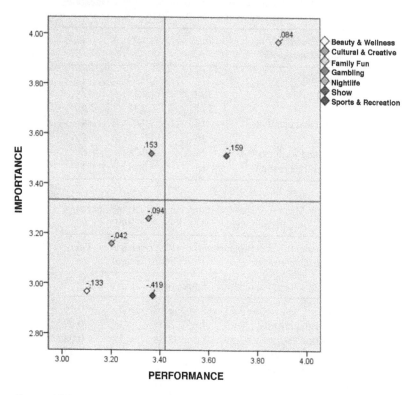

Figure 6.3 Important-Performance Analysis for entertainment products in Macau

the consumers. The only dimension where performance does not match the importance given by tourists is gaming.

Concentrate Here quadrant

The Concentrate Here quadrant captures a single dimension, gaming. Gaming includes horse racing, greyhound racing, lottery, and casino. However, according to Tables 6.2 and 6.3, out of the 199 respondents who experienced gaming, 188 of them experienced only casino. Only 11 responses were from the remaining three items. It is not hard to conclude that most of the people who experience gaming do so in casinos. This further confirms those who are worried about the extremely concentrated gaming industry in the casino.

Gaming was the second most important dimensions according to the respondents. However, the performance of it was only ranked in the middle.

These results suggest that the government should exert more effort to improve gaming and should pay special attention to underperformance. The reasons for the underperformance could be three folded. First, according to Lau (2014), 133 slot machine payouts were rejected due to "mechanical errors". In particular, a USD 20 million payout was rejected due to "mechanical errors" after USD 4 million was put into the slot machine. However, the USD 4 million was not refunded. This not only created a poor image of Macau casinos, but also a sense of unfairness to many gamblers around the world. Second, officially, the payout ratio of Macau casino slot machines should be around 80% to 98%. However, for older machines, the payout ratio can be as low as 70% (Stradbrooke, 2013). Alternatively, the payout ratio in Las Vegas is 99%, and there were few "mechanical errors" reported. Third, from the perspective of table games, the variety of games offered in Macau was far less than the number of games offered in Las Vegas. The list of table games in Macau included Baccarat, Blackjack, Craps, Sic Bo, American Roulette, Caribbean Stud Poker, Three-Card Poker, Money Wheel, and War; while Vegas, on top of the games offered in Macau, included Spanish 21, Pai Gow, Texas Shootout, Buster Blackjack, Flushes Gone Wild, King's Bounty Blackjack, Mississippi Stud, and many more. Although one might argue some of these games are just a small variation of the original games, one cannot deny the variety of excitement that casinos in Las Vegas bring to their customers. Hence, the performance of Macau casino gaming felt into the Concentrate Here region. Concerns should be raised, and gambling operators should introduce a larger variety for both slot and table games. Furthermore, slot machines should be checked more frequently to avoid mechanical errors. Sometimes, when there is a mechanical error, money put into the slot machine should be refunded at the least. From the government's perspective, tighter regulation should be imposed. For example, instead of receiving a lump sum profit from the gaming operators, regulators should look at the profit and loss of individual slot machines regularly.

Keep Up the Good Work quadrant

Two categories, family fun and shows, were located in the Keep Up the Good Work quadrant. Family fun includes museums, themed shopping, and themed dining. Among the 337 responses from family fun, 215 came from themed shopping, 81 came from themed dining, and 41 came from museums. The distribution was slightly concentrated toward themed shopping. Shows included popular concerts, classical concerts, and magic performances. Similar to the distribution of gaming, the distribution of shows was concentrated on a particular entertainment product. Out of the 171 responses from shows, 141 came from magic performances. Only 10 and 8 responses came from popular concerts and classical concerts respectively. However, this overly concentrated distribution could be caused by the fact that there were no special concerts when the researchers were collecting data. Furthermore, there was no singer who permanently stayed in Macau to perform, while there were several regularly scheduled shows, such as House of Dancing Water and House of Magic.

These categories were above average in importance and performance. This meant that the entertainment industry in Macau performed well in these categories. The performance of shows was slightly higher than the importance (0.16), while the performance of family fun was slightly lower than the importance (0.08). Efforts should be made to maintain the performance of the two categories, and there should be efforts to draw people's attention to other activities, such as theme dining and museums.

Low Priority quadrant

Four out of seven categories were located in the Low Priority quadrant. The dimensions were nightlife, beauty and wellness, sports and recreation, and culture and creative. It is usually recommended that few resources should be expended for dimensions in this low priority cell (Zhang & Chow, 2004). However, over 50% of the tourism products (in terms of category) promoted by the Macau Tourism Board or the Macau government are located in this quadrant. This means more than half of the tourism products are not valued by the customers. Furthermore, the entertainment product with the highest number of experiences within this quadrant was local art community, which was ranked five. The next in line were bars and lounges and spas, which were ranked seven and eight respectively. The remaining tourism products were experienced by less than 10 tourists. Given the low level of participation, government officials should consider whether these dimensions are worth promoting or whether there are problems with the current promotion methods.

Conclusion and recommendations

This study evaluated the importance and performance of the seven dimensions of entertainment products as suggested by the Macau Tourism Board. The results indicate that the entertainment products provided by the Macau tourism industry performed well in family fun and shows. In general, the entertainment products matched the importance level required by the tourists. Six out of seven of the categories provided by the entertainment industry in Macau felt into either the Low Priority quadrant or the Keep Up the Good Work quadrant. The only category that deviates was gaming. Furthermore, the gaming product was extremely concentrated in the casinos. Only 9 out of

308 tourists actually experienced other gaming entertainment products, such as greyhound racing and horse racing. This overconcentration could lead to an undiversified economy, which was not healthy to the development of Macau. This meant that the Macau government needed not only to diversify the types of industry in Macau but also to diversify within the gaming industry. Throughout the years, the chief executive of Macau had been advocating promoting Macau to develop into a "World Centre of Tourism and Leisure", and "Diversify Tourism Products" was one of the top goals (MGTO, 2016a). Efforts had been made to promote culture, MICE, shopping, and festivals since then. However, based on the results of this study, efforts to diversify within the gaming industry have underperformed. More resources should be devoted to improve existing alternative gaming activities and develop new gaming products to maintain the name "Las Vegas of the East".

Furthermore, the performance of Macau gaming entertainment products did not meet the importance levels of the tourists. Possible reasons could be casinos being "unfair" to the customers, in terms of not only the payout ratio, but also occasional mechanical errors. The Macau government should consider whether it should allow the casinos or gaming operators to regulate themselves or if the government should impose tighter regulations and more monitoring. Another possible reason for low performance on gaming could be due to the fact that the number of games offered by the Macau casinos was fewer than the corresponding casinos in Las Vegas. Given the recent financial crisis in China, and China as one of the most important sources of tourists, casino operators might want to consider diversifying the customer base. Since China prohibited gambling, Macau became the closest destination for many Chinese to gamble legally. However, tourists from other destinations, such as the United States, Europe, Singapore, and so on, could go to legal casinos locally. To attract these customers, the casino operators should create more gaming products.

The number of entertainment product categories that fell into the Low Priority quadrant should raise concerns to entertainment providers and the Macau government. On one hand, one could argue that the entertainment industry in Macau was efficient in the sense that they provided exactly what tourists valued. One the other hand, one could argue the diversification process, or the process of turning Macau into a "World Centre of Tourism and Leisure", was not successful. Tourist participation in many other entertainment products was low. The question to the entertainment providers is whether they should be satisfied with the level of products they are currently providing. As mentioned in the introduction section, the number of nightclubs, bars, karaoke clubs, and discos was growing rapidly in China. This means that nightlife is attractive to many Chinese people, who were also the main customer base of Macau. Tourism practitioners, such as tour guides or the Macau Tourism Board, should cooperate with entertainment providers to promote alternative entertainment products to tourists. Furthermore, from the government perspective, the results of this study also indicate many tourists visit Macau with a single purpose, gambling. The government should promote diversified entertainment activities for overseas tourists and to enhance the image of Macau.

This study provides several contributions. This study contributes to the tourism and hospitality literature by summarizing the categories of entertainment products. Moreover, this study enhances knowledge on entertainment products in the tourism and hospitality literature. This study identifies the importance and performance of the entertainment connotation for the customers in a gaming destination. This research discovers the important entertainment products among tourists.

Furthermore, this study provides several contributions related to application. First, from the government perspective, this study discovered that themed shopping and casino were the most important entertainment products. Given the importance of themed shopping and its current performance, the government should provide more corresponding entertainment products, such as a shopping mall with various themes, elements, and style. For example, there are various fashion shows within the shopping malls in Las Vegas. Second, themed dining was also identified as an important entertainment product. The government could focus on the dining culture, especially the Portuguese dining culture. As the government has tried to diversify the tourism products in Macau, dining has become an attractive product to tourists. Third, the least important and least performance entertainment products were nightlife, beauty and wellness, sports and recreation, and culture and creative. From the government point of view, either the government should increase promotions abroad or should reposition the entertainment product.

From the gambling operator point of view, this study shows that casinos should provide more diverse gaming products, enhance the experience of the tourists, and hence increase the satisfaction provided by the entertainment experience. This study could also serve as a marketing tool for other entertainment providers. Entertainment providers could design corresponding entertainment products according to the preferences of tourists and increase their market shares and competitiveness.

Limitations and future research

Some limitations need to be addressed. First, most of the respondents in this study were Chinese. People from a different culture would have different perceptions on entertainment products and tourism products. Hence, this study focused on Chinese culture, which could potentially limit the generalizability of its research findings. Further research could incorporate a more diversified data sample to examine whether the findings from this study are replicable. Second, seasonality of entertainment would affect the results. For example, if we collected the data during November, which was when the Grand Prix was held, there would be a bigger proportion of people visiting Macau for sports entertainment. Future research might conduct a panel data survey, incorporating the longitude aspect of data. Third, our research focused on tourism products, and we did not consider service attributes and the tourists' experience. Future research could incorporate entertainment service and quality and tourists' experience in the study.

In conclusion, this study intended to study the importance and performance of entertainment products in Macau. This study represents one of the first studies on entertainment products for tourists' experiences. The tourism and entertainment industry is an important component in the world's service sector, and entertainment tourism deserves more scholarly attention for future research.

References

Adeboye, C. A. (2012). *The impact of entertainment on tourism. Case study: Agency Remarc in Greece.* Central Ostrobothnia University of Applied. Retrieved on 20 June 2016, from www.theseus.fi/bitstream/handle/10024/47217/Adeboye_Christopher. pdf?sequence=1

Besciu, I. G. (2013). Behavior of the consumer of tourist entertainment services. *Cactus Tourism Journal, 4*(2), 9–19.

Blanke, J., & Chiesa, T. (2013). *The travel and tourism competitiveness report 2013.* World Economic Forum. Retrieved on 20 June 2016, from www3.weforum.org/docs/WEF_TT_Competitiveness_Report_2013.pdf

Bond, P. (2013). *Study: Global media industry poised to top $2 trillion in 2016.* Retrieved on 20 June 2016, from www.hollywoodreporter.com/news/study-global-media-industry-poised-562694

Chang, H. L., & Yang, C. H. (2008). Do airline self-service check-in kiosks meet the needs of passengers? *Tourism Management, 29*(5), 980–993.

Chen, C. (2012). Hierarchical linear relationship between the U.S. leisure and entertainment consumption. *Technology in Society, 34*(1), 44–54. Retrieved from http://dx.doi.org/10.1016/j.techsoc.2011.12.003

Cirque du Soleil. (2016). *Press room.* Retrieved on 01 July 2016, from www. cirquedusoleil.com/en/press/kits/corporate/cirque-du-soleil/history.aspx

Cohen, M. (2011, June 30). Macau needs decades to go beyond gambling. *Asia Time Online.* Retrieved on 01 July 2016, from www.atimes.com/atimes/Southeast_Asia/MF30Ae02.html

Deng, W. (2007). Using a revised importance-performance analysis approach: The case of Taiwanese hot springs tourism. *Tourism Management, 28*(5), 1274–1284.

Frauman, E., & Banks, S. (2011). Gateway community resident perceptions of tourism development: Incorporating importance-performance analysis into a limits of acceptable change framework. *Tourism Management, 32*(31), 128–140.

Galaxy Entertainment. (2004, June 23). *Galaxy launches entertainment business in Macau. Actively promotes local tourism and economic development. Rollout first project Galaxy Waldo. Begins construction of Galaxy Star World by end of June. And conceptual plans for Cotai mega resort have been submitted.* Retrieved on 02 February 2016, from www.galaxyentertainment.com/uploads/investor/92_2Yuma.pdf

Global Gaming Expo Asia. (2015, January 16). Global Gaming Expo (G2E) Asia announces new pavilion for nightlife and entertainment, partners with Macau International Clubbing Show (MICS). *G2E Asia Press Release.* Retrieved on 02 February 2016, from www.g2easia.com/News-Press/Press-Release/Global-Gaming-Expo-G2E-Asia-Announces-New-Pavilion-for-Nightlife-and-Entertainment-Partners-with-Macau-International-Clubbing-Show-MICS/

Gunn, C. A. (1988). *Tourism planning,* 2nd ed. New York: Taylor and Francis.

Hansen, E., & Bush, R. (1999). Understanding customer quality requirements: Model and application. *Industrial Marketing Management, 28*(2), 119–130.

Hospitality Industry Education Advisory Committee. (2016). *Entertainment and tourism.* Retrieved on 02 February 2016, from www.go2hr.ca/bc-tourism-industry/what-tourism/recreation-and-entertainment

Hughes, H. (2000). *Arts, entertainment and tourism.* Oxford: Butterworth Heinemann.

Hughes, H., & Benn, D. (1997). Tourism and cultural policy: The case of seaside entertainment in Britain. *European Journal of Cultural Policy, 3*(2), 235–255.

Joppe, M., Martin, D. W., & Waalen, J. (2001). Toronto's image as a destination: A comparative importance-satisfaction analysis by origin of visitor. *Journal of Travel Research, 39,* 252–260.

Lau, S. (2014, July 16). *Macau casinos withhold 133 slot machine payouts claiming wins were due to 'mechanical errors'.* Retrieved on 20 June 2016, from www.scmp.com/news/china/article/1555051/macau-slot-players-protest-being-denied-winnings

Linda, S. L., & To, W. M. (2010). Importance-performance analysis for public management decision making: An empirical study of China's special administrative region. *Management Decision, 48*(2), 277–295. Retrieved from http://dx.doi.org/10.1108/00251741011022626

Loi, K. I., & Pearce, P. L. (2012). Powerful stakeholders' views of entertainment in Macao's future. *Journal of Business Research, 65*(1), 4–12.

Macao Government Public Security Police Force Headquarters (FSM). (2016). *Entry and exit of non-residents.* Retrieved on 01 August 2016, from www.fsm.gov.mo/psp/eng/EDoN.html

Macao Government Tourism Office (MGTO). (2016a). *Macao tourism industry development master plan.* Retrieved on 01 July 2016, from http://primary-usergroup.simpleviewcms.com/flipbooks/en/files/inc/02958b1f1e.pdf

Macao Government Tourism Office (MGTO). (2016b). *Shows & entertainment.* Retrieved on 01 July 2016, from http://en.macaotourism.gov.mo/showentertainment/showentertainment.php?c=1

Macao Statistics and Census Bureau (DSEC). (2016a). *Tourism and gaming.* Retrieved on 01 July 2016, from www.dsec.gov.mo/default.aspx#

Macao Statistics and Census Bureau (DSEC). (2016b). *Company statistics.* Retrieved on 01 July 2016, from www.dsec.gov.mo/TimeSeriesDatabase.aspx

Martilla, J. A., & James, J. C. (1977). Importance-performance analysis. *The journal of marketing,* 77–79.

Matzler, K., Bailom, F., Hinterhuber, H. H., Renzl, B., & Pichler, J. (2004). The asymmetric relationship between attribute-level performance and overall customer satisfaction: A reconsideration of the importance-performance analysis. *Industrial Marketing Management, 33,* 271–277.

McCarthy, J. (2002). Entertainment-led regeneration: The case of Detroit. *Cities, 19*(2), 105–111.

Melco Crown Entertainment. (2016). *About us.* Retrieved on 01 July 2016, from www.melco-crown.com/eng/bg.php

Murphy, P. E. (1985). *Tourism: A community approach.* London: Methuen.

O'Leary, S., & Deegan, J. (2005). Ireland's image as a tourism destination in France: Attribute importance and performance. *Journal of Travel Research, 43*(3), 47–256.

Pearce, P., & Loi, K.-I. (2012). Powerful stakeholders' views of entertainment in Macao's future. *Journal of Business Research, 65*(1), 4–12.

Pritchard, M., & Havitz, M. (2006). Destination appraisal: An analysis of critical incidents. *Annals of Tourism Research, 33*(1), 25–46.

PRLog. (2013, June 5). *Dancing for diversification: Macau.com on Macau's entertainment trends.* Retrieved on 20 June 2016, from www.prlog.org/12150802-dancing-for-diversification-macaucom-on-macaus-entertainment-trends.html

Robinson, P., Lück, M., Smith, S. L., & Lackey, M. (Eds.). (2013). *Tourism.* CABI.

Shifflet, D. K. (1992). Bringing in the business travelers. *Hotel & Resort Industry, 15*(11), 66–72.

Smith, S. L. (1994). The tourism product. *Annals of Tourism Research, 21*(3), 582–595.

Sorensson, A., & Friedrichs, Y. (2013). An importance-performance analysis of sustainable tourism: A comparison between international and national tourists. *Journal of Destination Marketing and Management, 2,* 14–21.

Stănciulescu, G., & Jugănaru, I. D. (2006). *Entertainment and entertainer in tourism.* Bucharest: Uranus Publishing House.

Stradbrooke, S. (2013, November 30). *Record jackpots as slots gain favor with Macau casino gamblers.* Retrieved on 20 June 2016, from http://calvinayre.com/2013/11/30/casino/record-jackpots-slots-gain-favor-macau-casino-gamblers/

Tonge, J., & Moore, S. A. (2007). Importance-satisfaction analysis for marine-park hinterlands: A Western Australian case study. *Tourism Management, 28*(3), 768–776.

UNWTO. (2016). *UNWTO world tourism barometer.* Retrieved on 20 June 2016, from http://media.unwto.org/press-release/2016-01-18/international-tourist-arrivals-4-reach-record-12-billion-2015

Wu, H. H., & Shieh, J. I. (2009). The development of a confidence interval-based importance-performance analysis by considering variability in analyzing service quality. *Expert Systems With Applications, 36*(3), 7040–7044. Retrieved from http://dx.doi.org/10.1016/j.eswa.2008.08.055

Wu, H. H., & Shieh, J. I. (2010). Quantifying uncertainty in applying importance-performance analysis. *Quality and Quantity, 44,* 997–1003. Retrieved from http:// dx.doi.org/10.1007/s11135-009-9245-8

Xu, J. B. (2010). Perception of tourism products. *Tourism Management, 31,* 607–610.

Yavas, U., & Shemwell, D. J. (2001). Modified importance-performance analysis: An application to hospitals. *International Journal of Health Care Quality Assurance, 14*(3), 104–110. Retrieved from http://dx.doi.org/10.1108/09526860110391568

Zhang, H. Q., & Chow, I. (2004). Application of importance-performance model in tour guides' performance: Evidence from mainland Chinese outbound visitors in Hong Kong. *Tourism Management, 25,* 81–91.

Index

amenities 5, 18–20, 29
American Indian 11
art performance 1, 42
attractions i, 1–5, 10–11, 14–15, 23–24, 29, 33, 36–37, 40, 43, 45–46
Australia 4, 42, 49

bars 3, 5–6, 17–18, 23, 32, 42, 48, 52, 56–57
beauty and wellness 21, 23, 25, 46, 48, 53, 56, 58
bird watching, 2, 29, 42
Broadway musical 12

casino 1, 3, 5, 9–11, 13–14, 17–19, 23–24, 29–31, 33, 37, 46, 48, 52–58
China i, 12–13, 21, 23–25, 33, 36–37, 42–46, 49–50, 57
Chinese tourists 25
cinema 2, 5, 17
circus 3, 11, 44
Cirque du Soleil 11–12, 14, 18, 44
comedy 3
concerts vii, 1, 3–5, 17, 30, 42, 45–46, 48, 52, 55–56
consumer behaviours 29–30, 34
cultural and creative industries zones 21–22, 25
cultural features 32

dance performance 1, 23, 42
destination, i, viii, 1–4, 10, 12, 14, 17, 24–25, 29, 31, 35–36, 40, 42–43, 45, 47, 57–58
destination management 31, 34

disco 17–18, 32, 42, 57
distractions 2
diving 29
downtown 9

economic 1, 4, 29–30, 37, 42
entertainment activities viii, 2–4, 21, 42, 48, 58
entertainment industry viii, 2–3, 6, 10–12, 17–18, 25, 29, 33, 36–37, 42–44, 56–57, 59
entertainment product i, viii, 1–3, 25, 33, 39, 43–46, 48, 52–59
entertainment zones 5–6
Europe 4, 12, 17, 38, 42, 57
exhibits 3, 5, 10, 21–22, 31, 35, 38, 39, 51
experience i, viii, 1, 3–4, 6, 10, 17–18, 28, 35–36, 39–40, 42–43, 45–46, 48, 52–54, 56–59

family fun 9, 11, 21–22, 25, 31–32, 46, 48, 52–53, 55–56
Finland 5
fishing 2, 29, 42
full service theory 19

Galaxy Entertainment Group 13, 48
gambling viii, 1, 4, 9, 11, 13, 17, 19, 31, 33, 36, 38, 42–44, 55, 57–58
games viii, 2, 6, 23, 29, 35, 43, 45, 55, 57
Gaming Inspection and Coordination Bureau 33
golfing 2, 29, 32, 42, 48, 52
Grand Prix 34, 59

greyhound racing 23, 48, 52–54, 57
Guangdong 12–14, 21, 33, 37, 43
Guangzhou 37

Hong Kong 6, 12–13, 21, 23, 33, 37, 43, 45, 49–50
horse racing 17, 23, 48, 52–54, 57
horse riding 2, 17, 23, 29, 42, 48, 52–54, 57
Hospitality Industry Education Advisory Committee 2, 43
House of Dancing Water 20–21, 44, 56
Howard Hughes 9

India 12, 38
industrial management 33
infrastructure resources 32
IPA analysis viii, 46–47, 53
Italy 5

Japan 12, 33, 49–50
justification 19

karaoke clubs 17, 42, 57

Lan Kwai Fong 6
Las Vegas i, viii, 3–5, 9–14, 17–18, 24, 43–44, 46, 55, 57–58
Las Vegas Convention and Visitors Authority 4, 9–10
license 13
London 5–6
lottery 48, 52, 54

Macao's Statistics and Census Service 12
Macau Tower 22, 46
magic performance viii, 1, 4, 30, 42, 48, 52, 55
Malaysia 18
Melco 13, 44
MGM 4, 10, 12–13, 18, 23–24, 44
monopoly 13
museums 1–3, 5, 10, 18, 29–30, 45, 48, 52, 55–56
musicals viii, 3–5, 12, 30, 32
music and medieval festivals 3

Nevada 9
New York 12
nightclub 3–5, 10, 17–18, 21, 23, 42, 44, 46, 57
nightlife 3, 5–6, 9–10, 17, 21, 23, 25, 31–32, 42, 46–48, 53, 56–58
non-gaming 14–15, 18–20, 24, 46

one belt one road 37
online media 28

Pearl River Delta (PRD) 12–13
Philippines 18, 43
pool parties 3, 10, 44, 46
Portugal 12
pubs 5, 17

recreation 2, 21, 23, 25, 29, 31–32, 42, 46, 48, 53, 56, 58
regulating tourists 33
resource management 31

Sands 13, 37
Shenzhen 33
shows 1, 3–5, 9–10, 12, 14, 17–19, 21, 24–25, 31, 42, 44–48, 53, 55–56, 58
Singapore 4, 18, 20–21, 24, 42–43, 45, 57
skiing 29
slogan 9
smartphones 28
social media 24, 28
Sociedade de Turismo e Diversoes de Macau (STDM) 13
Soho 5–6
South Korea 18, 21, 33, 43, 45, 49–50
spillover effects 19
sport events 2–3
sport and recreation 21, 23, 25, 46, 48, 53, 56, 58
streaming video 28
street performance 3, 5, 46
The Strip 9–10
sustainable development 44

Taiwan 21, 33, 37, 43, 45, 49–50
talk shows 1, 42
theme parks 2–3, 9–10, 29, 36, 39, 46
tourism development i, viii, 17, 20,
    36–37, 40
tourism industry viii, 1, 4, 6, 10, 25, 29,
    37–38, 42–43, 53, 56
tourism resources 31, 35, 37, 39

United Kingdom 5
United States 3–5, 9, 18, 42, 49, 57

Vietnam 18
virtual reality i, 3, 35–36,
    39–40, 46

World Bank 13
Wynn Macau 13–14

youth market 39

ZAIA 21, 44–45
Zhuhai 12, 37